In a Homeland Not Far

Also by Yahya Frederickson

The Gold Shop of Ba-'Ali
The Birds of al-Merjeh Square: Poems from Syria (chapbook)
Month of Honey, Month of Missiles (chapbook)
Returning to Water (chapbook)

In a Homeland Not Far

—— New & Selected Poems ——

Yahya Frederickson

Press 53
Winston-Salem

Press 53, LLC
PO Box 30314
Winston-Salem, NC 27130

First Edition

Silver Concho Poetry Series

Cover design by Kevin Morgan Watson

Cover art, "Step Well, Jaipur," Copyright © 2016 by Yahya Frederickson, used by permission of the artist.

Author photo by Fathia Ali

Printed on acid-free paper
ISBN 978-1-941209-54-7

for Fathia, Ama, and Abdu

Acknowledgments

The author thanks the editors of the following journals for publishing poems in this collection, or earlier versions of them:

Arts & Letters: "The Barber of Taiwan," "From the *Gari*"

Black Warrior Review: "Matmata"

Crab Orchard Review: "Sacrifice," "Strolling in Béja, the Eve of *al-Maulid*"

The Cream City Review: "Cattle from Ethiopia"

Cutthroat: "The Bus to Aden," "Conspiracy Theory," "The Gold Shop of Ba-'Ali," "Oriental Batman"

Flyway: "Praying beside the *Mujahed*"

Hanging Loose: "Curing"

Lake Region Review: "Carthage," "Holiday Lights"

The Laurel Review: "*Chott el-Djerid*" (formerly titled "Crossing *Chott el-Djerid*")

Luna: "Letter from Addis Ababa," "Letter from aboard the Djibouti-Addis Train," "Letter from Negash"

Al-Masar: "All-Night Teashop," "*Duqq*"

Mizna: "What I Learn about Poetry in Syria" (formerly titled "Poetry Lesson [Syria]")

Ninth Letter: "Festival of Sacrifice," "Hussam's Heart"

Quarter After Eight: "Secession"

Quarterly West: "Letter from Dessie," "Letter from Harar"

Red Cedar: "Badria," "First Breakfast," "*Bet Rimbo*," "Gypsy Camp," "The Donkey" (originally titled "Pastorale")

Red Weather: "Letter from Damascus [to Mark Vinz]," "Letter from Hama [to Sameer]," "My Beautiful Syrian Students Practice Their Cursive"

River Styx: "Letter from Alemata," "Letter from Hayq," "Requiem for al-Mocha"

The Southern Review: "Can"

Water~Stone Review: "Letter from Damascus [to Thom Tammaro]"

Witness: "The Messiah of Kogi State" (formerly titled "Letters from Kogi")

Thanks also to the following presses and their editors: Lost Horse Press for publishing *The Gold Shop of Ba-'Ali* (2014); Finishing Line Press for publishing *The Birds of al-Merjeh Square: Poems from Syria* (2014); Tigertail Productions for publishing *Month of Honey, Month of Missiles* (2009).

Contents

Introduction
Yahya Frederickson

In 1989 the streets of Sana'a, the capital of North Yemen, were still sleepy. Each day I walked them across town to Sana'a University, where I taught English courses as a Peace Corps volunteer. Tall and Nordic, I was glaringly out of place. Students dubbed me *al-Ziraafa*—"the Giraffe"—for the way I strode slowly and stooped under the low branches of the trees flanking the campus sidewalks. Yet nowhere else had I felt I belonged more.

Something inside me was starting to make sense. Something in the faces—a different beauty, an exuberance, a hopefulness, a dignity wrought by history. Something in the hospitality showered upon total strangers, something in the aromatic hubbub of the *souq*; in the prayer call rolling like a giant wave over the Old City, which according to legend was founded by a son of Noah, and over al-Qaa', the precinct of sunken homes in which Sana'a's Jewish population had lived until Operation Magic Carpet airlifted them to Israel in the late 1940s, and on, and on.

I grew up in northern Minnesota, in a horizontal town hemmed in by a patchwork quilt of sugar beets, sunflowers, and soybeans. Yet what I wanted was the world. I wanted to see its history, its strife, even its drudgery. Though most of my friends moved to the Twin Cities, I attended college down the street, where my father taught. I studied anthropology, world literature, international political thought, world religions. The more I learned, the more I wanted to leave. My new college friends could see that if I stayed, I would suffocate. And so I did leave, to the Pacific Northwest as an exchange student, out East briefly, then to Montana for grad school. With a fresh MFA in Creative Writing, I wasn't exactly inundated with job offers, so I applied for the Peace Corps. Finally, a call came from a Peace Corps regional office: "Would you be interested in serving in Yemen?"

Could I think it over for a while? Yes, the Peace Corps officer said, of course. Great, I thought, at least then I could look up which continent Yemen was on. And when I asked a professor friend of mine, who seemed to know about every country on Earth, what I should do, he said, "Go. You'll love it." Ancient culture. Tribal traditions. Limited Western encroachment.

So I went.

In 1990, several months after my arrival, while East and West Germany were reunifying, so were North and South Yemen. During Reunification celebrations, Sana'a's Tahrir Square pulsed with many small circles of men in white gowns, jackets, and turbans dancing the *bara'*, a traditional dance of stepping and whirling in mirror image of each other, their *janbia* daggers glinting in the air while drummers pattered their shallow drums.

That year, I fasted the Islamic month of Ramadan. When my American colleagues found out, their jaws dropped: "Why would you do such a thing? Are you going native?" I was fasting to demonstrate my cultural sensitivity, I told them, to be on the same energy level as my students and everyone else in this country in which we are guests. I wasn't always sure when was the time to stop eating my pre-dawn meal. Those long, haunting prayers moaning from the mosque loudspeakers—were they pre-prayer supplications, or were they the prayer itself?

I'll not forget a particular morning about halfway through the month. As usual, I was sitting in the whitewashed kitchen of my centuries-old, six-story stone house in the Old City, my meal done. But as I sat there, watching the sky lighten through the window, a new feeling came over me: what I was doing felt *right*. For the first time I could remember, I was not worried about my future. A road beckoned. I borrowed a Qur'an from a friend and began reading.

But the world always encroaches. My two-year commitment to the Peace Corps was interrupted by the first Gulf War, Operation Desert Storm. Still smarting from the Iranian hostage crisis, my government decided to play it safe, suspending the Peace Corps program and repatriating its volunteers. "Teacher," a student said to me before I left, "don't worry, you can stay with my family. We will protect you." And I knew what he said was true.

Back in Minnesota, what would happen to my new sense of belonging? Would it shrivel away? Would I feel ashamed, like after an impossibly happy dream? Actually, my evacuation from Yemen provided the perfect acid test. Plunked back into my childhood home, I found that my interest in Islam only grew. My parents and I watched news footage of Operation Desert Storm—the charred getaway cars scuttled on the highway to Iraq, the Kuwaiti oilfields ablaze, the yellow ribbons tied around tree trunks in America. But I knew more of the background now: the legacy of borders drawn by colonialism, America's schizophrenic relations with despots, and America's addiction to oil.

I continued to read my Qur'an. I stopped Arabic speakers in shops, startling them with my *as-salaamu 'alaykum*. They pointed me to a rented apartment-turned-makeshift mosque near the university. I asked questions. I learned the movements of the five daily prayers and practiced them behind my bedroom door. Once time, my mother walked in with some clean laundry for me while I was prostrating on the floor. Perhaps the time to convert was near.

I admired Islam's powerful simplicity: there is a Creator, and the rest is creation. I read more, rediscovering many of the names I'd known from Sunday school: Noah, Abraham, Moses, Mary, Jesus, and others. From my new text, their exemplary lives still spoke to me: *do what's right; be kind; treat others as you'd want to be treated; don't lose hope; don't stop caring.*

And when at last I repeated the *shihada*, or statement of faith, in the apartment of two international students, it was somewhat anticlimactic. For me, the change had been on the horizon for some time already. But there I was, officially a Muslim.

Though it's not a requirement, I wanted a new first name to reflect my new identity, a name not only meaningful but also— because of my long last name—brief. I chose Yahya, a name common in Yemen due to one of its last kings, Imam Yahya. Yahya is the Arabic form of John, the figure known to Christians as John the Baptist. In the Qur'an Yahya is described as wise, compassionate to all creatures, devout, dutiful to parents, and humble. When I wrote my new initials in English, I liked the way the straight strokes of *Y* and *F* slanted and cantilevered; when I wrote them in Arabic, I liked the way the Arabic equivalents *ya* and *fa* looped and rolled. Though the two-syllable name with an aspirated *H* in the middle would prove nearly impossible for non-Arabic speakers to pronounce, my last name would be equally impossible for Arabic speakers. Sometimes, I appreciate the "teachable moment" it provides. But regardless of how I feel about it on any given day, my Arabic first name and Norwegian surname represent me more accurately than anything: I straddle two worlds.

After military actions in the Gulf ran their course in 1991, I returned to Yemen with my new identity. Sana'a had also changed: hundreds of thousands of Yemeni workers had been expelled from Saudi Arabia due to political fallout, and judging from Sana'a's honking, congested streets, I'd guess that each of those workers drove a used car back from the Kingdom. The mosques I used to walk past, some of which dated back to the first centuries after the Prophet Muhammad, I now entered and prayed in. A reluctant celebrity, I met *imam*s and Islamic scholars, some of whom spoke English better than I spoke Arabic. I prayed next to smiling *mujahedeen* who had fought in the 1980s and '90s to expel the Soviets from Afghanistan and had returned home with—at least briefly—unbridled optimism.

After completing the second year of my two-year Peace Corps commitment, I didn't want to leave. I took various teaching jobs, and after a couple years met and married Fathia. A few weeks into our marriage, the frayed union of North and South Yemen finally snapped: evenings we spent huddling in our neighbor's stairwell, waiting for the blast of the solitary Scud missile, the retort of anti-aircraft artillery. The secessionist movement was crushed, but not without cost.

A year later, Fathia gave birth to twins, born almost hopelessly premature, but nursed at home in gauze-covered cribs rather than in hospital incubators, which, due to frequent power outages, served more effectively as coffins. Our babies survived and grew strong.

By 1996, phone calls to my parents revealed that they were experiencing more complicated health problems. Fathia, who had already lost both parents, said, "You have to help them. It's your duty as a Muslim." So we returned to Minnesota.

While I was away, my home state of Minnesota had become home to thousands of Somali refugees fleeing their country's civil war. Seeing a traditionally dressed Somali family walking around downtown Fargo in search of an apartment, I couldn't help but feel happy that the Red Sea region had followed me home.

Over the years, I have traveled whenever and wherever possible. Brief visits to Tunisia, Ethiopia, Turkey, and Morocco. Shortly after 9/11, I traveled to Mecca to perform the *hajj*, one of the five pillars of faith, in which pilgrims recount through various stations the history of monotheism from Abraham to Muhammad. Later that year, I visited Nigeria with a team of teachers hired by a Nigerian governor to "assess the curriculum" of his state's university. Did our visit have anything to do with his bid for reelection? Furthermore, I've been blessed with three Fulbright Scholar awards, allowing me the opportunity to live and work in Syria in 2005, Saudi Arabia in 2011, and Kyrgyzstan in 2016. A day rarely passes when I don't dream of being elsewhere—a mountaintop village, an oasis town, the labyrinth of an ancient city. A romantic view, to be sure, but one I find difficult to escape.

In a well-known *hadeeth*, the Prophet Muhammad advises, "Be in this world as a stranger or a wayfarer." This has become my mantra, for we can never go home, we can never go back in time. The world changes, and we do too, as we step towards the unknown. The best we can do is to observe, contemplate, and move on.

We belong nowhere, and everywhere.

With these poems I invite you along.

Y. F. ي ف

YEMEN

CAN

Sana'a University

Can a can can a can? the students of linguistics quiz me, giggling as if they've heard the most delicious gossip. They are students of Dr. D. Thakur, or D.T., the Indian professor who has been teaching here since the university was built. With his thick glasses, Brylcreemed silver hair, and calm demeanor, he's as guru as can be in a country of Muslims. Surrounded by his disciples in the inner sanctum of his flat, he claps his hands and says, *Madame, sweets.* His wife parts the curtain, setting before them a tray of petit-fours and tamarind juice.

Can a can can a can? they bubble. Late for my own lecture, I'm walking past the Faculty of Science, where the skeleton of a whale or huge fish, probably from the Red Sea, is displayed. It must be similar to whatever swallowed Yunus, the claustrophobic story familiar to all People of the Book. Behind me, the hedges of red geraniums are in bloom. Oh, to be the lucky gardener of the university grounds, day in and day out slaking the thirst of things that blossom and bear fruit! No wonder young women sit on the benches nearby, drawing Seven-Up from cool green bottles, through bright plastic straws, to their lips.

Can a can can a can? they keep asking, and I'm guessing it must be a grammatical miracle, a secret code they expect I know. What I do know is it's a question I'll never ask. Beyond their silly grins, I notice male students at the main gate surrendering their daggers to the soldier. They'll get the daggers back after class. Last year during final exams, the soldier's pet buzzard, loose from its tether, hopped into my classroom. My students slapped its beak with their test papers until it squawked and, like I do when confounded by a puzzle, flapped away.

DUQQ

I believe only the desert
can know the aridity
of cardamom, coffee, and ginger.

In his small *diwan*,
Firas and I sip *duqq*
with his distant relatives,

who have come from their village
for medicine, work, or maybe
an official stamp. I don't pry.

On the poster above my head
Saddam Hussein atop a white stallion
waves to a clapping throng.

A cousin asks
about America's motives
as if I am my country, and he his.

My Arabic, tinder-dry,
heats the room.
But from the kitchen,

Firas's mother is listening.
She hears me ask
about the drink she prepared.

I sip until the faces
of relatives eclipse
and it's time to excuse myself.

As I thank him, Firas presses
an aromatic sack into my hand
and recites the instructions

his mother gave him
to give me
for steeping the night.

ALL-NIGHT TEASHOP

Having tallied the day's cracks,
Majnoon sleeps on the sidewalk
with his soiled blanket and tin can.

A *qat* chewer spits his desires into the street,
orders a glass of milk tea,
strokes the softness of his own cheek.

Inside, behind a squad of blenders,
the sandwich boy furrows out
the soft guts of a bun.

Beyond the lone fluorescent bulb,
an army transport rattles to a halt,
emptying its cargo of young conscripts.

Their carbines sleep across their laps
as they devour sandwiches of jam
and cheese, glasses of mango juice.

And what am I? Not tourist,
not spy, not oil man looking to hire.
I offer no opportunities, nothing,

except maybe the compassion
I feel when I see, no greater
wish in the world than tea.

ON SABIR MOUNTAIN

Ta'izz

After tea, Mr. Mohandas asks if I would like to ascend. He must check the progress of the development project today. I follow him downstairs, where the servant who brought us tea is now the chauffeur poised at the wheel of the company Land Rover. We drive up, past the house of the man rich enough to demand the city's asphalt streets meet him at his gate, then up the dusty switchbacks until Ta'izz shrinks into the valley. On the slope a group of stonecutters ties a block on a man's back so he can walk it down. They offer us tea from the one small glass they share, but we decline. Up, up, we cut through terraced fields. The women of this mountain are storied. Proud as queens, they depend on no man to provide. In marriage, they command the highest dowries in the land, their lips grinning around teeth of gold! The Land Rover turns into the construction site, splitting the crowd that has already gathered. By the way the hand of Mr. Mohandas is shaken and kissed, I can tell the visit will take time. In the valley far below, the city has all but submerged. The only sounds are a water pump's chugging diesel, and laughter—for a cluster of young girls has spotted me. Already they know how little I comprehend. Village-bright, their dresses billow in the wind, so I ask *mumkin surah*, maybe a photograph? But they shrink away, hiding their mouths with the ends of their scarves, as their mothers would do. In a few years, suitors will ruin themselves for their small hands. Uphill, Mr. Mohandas motions me to return. The inspection is complete. During our long idle down, everything is as silent as time. Occasionally, I see an iridescent lizard warming itself on a stone. Down, down, into the city's loftiest precinct, where children frolic in the streets, swishing their shirts and shawls through the air. It is not a greeting for us, but for the diaphanous insects that they are catching in the folds. To my surprise, they bite with glee into each abdomen, which, like this day, is swollen with indescribable nectar.

REQUIEM FOR AL-MOCHA

for J.L.

Long gone the coffee, the storehouses
reeking of cinnamon, saffron, incense.
We walk the barren coast as clouds
crash and try to rain salt. They can't.

For 300 years, brick has been sinking,
rows of black stones askew in grit,
houses of dead merchants reduced
to rafters gray goats clitter across.

Minaret or lighthouse, rubble is rubble,
the barber reasons, swigging smuggled whiskey
in his shop's solitary chair. Ships
bring him more bottles than heads.

Every night, the landlady sleepwalks
up the stairs, stands in your doorway,
stares out from beneath the yellow bulb.
Her family escaped, but she's afraid to hate.

Even babies born dry and hard as dolls
fight for this life. Perhaps the placentas
mothers bury in sand do bring luck.
Luck of your hands, of any history at all.

CATTLE FROM ETHIOPIA

Relentless as minutes,
the sea stampedes the brim
of a rickety Djibouti ship.
In the night's warm waves,
cows know only east, and swim.
Today they rest like uprooted palms.

Stare into an open bovine eye
as crabs tunnel through flesh, orifice
to orifice, clicking diligent mandible
against mandible, crabs
exiting in panicked battalions,
poking eyestalks from sloping foam.

How many teeth to make a necklace?
What could be done with horn,
should it twist loose?
In a homeland not far,
people roll onto shore
with gaping holes.

A soldier offers
mango juice, sandwich cookies,
cigarettes. He's returning
to his village of thatch and fish
where children, in hot sand,
bury everything they hear.

THE BUS TO ADEN

stops in a village whose name
no one knows. Time for lunch.
In the seats in front of me,
passengers stir from their naps,
from their dreams of what traveling brings,
and stagger down the bus steps
then up the cement steps
into the open-front restaurant,

which fills instantly. The family
of waiters echoes our orders back
to the kitchen: trays of flaky bread,
tin plates of rice, sheep heads
yellowing in broth. After the meal,
our throats blossom with sweet red tea.
Though I try to consume quickly,

I am the last back on board, where
passengers have begun swapping
shopping stories, crinkling baby clothes
encased in cellophane, smoothing the bolts
of cloth bought for aunts. I can tell
our driver is from Aden, for his free hand
speaks with an excitement only subversives have.
Something must always be brought home.

THE LAST TIME

The last time I hang out with Ahmad is after we've been at a teashop, talking about music over milky tea. I'm feeling sleepy, but Ahmad says, *The night is still early. I've got two guitars at home, and my wife and children are out of town.* I cave, so we walk to his flat. At the gate, a car is parked. *Oh no,* he mutters. *Salih.*

Inside, we're met by Ahmad's older cousin Salih, an officer in the military. Another cousin, I forget his name, is there too, sitting in the corner of the *diwan,* his cheek bulging with *qat,* his hand busy with a cigarette. And at the other end of the room, a woman sits on the floor. She is poised like an empress, her back straight, her smile confident. She is dressed in a gown of turquoise satin, and her hair is wrapped in a scarf of sparkling gold. All of us sit before her in silent adoration.

Salih leaves the room. When he returns, he is no longer wearing his olive uniform but a white terrycloth bathrobe, his belly protruding over the cinched belt. Our presence will not alter his objective. I cringe to picture it. Our queen looks too fresh to be a prostitute, too comfortable to be a victim. For her delights, how much will he pay?

Salih glares at us. We've wasted too much of his time. The thinner cousin is staying put in his corner, maybe to watch, maybe to wait his own sloppy turn. Ahmad leads me out of the *diwan* and down the hall, to a small room whose shelves are stacked high with American CDs, whose cushions cradle two guitars. I start a slow blues shuffle while Ahmad thumb-strums something sad and Spanish. Our songs don't merge. We try a Bob Dylan tune that both of us know, but even that is hopeless: inside the room closed tight as a small fist, our discordant notes crumble onto the floor. We can't even keep time anymore.

WHAT I LEARN ABOUT POETRY IN YEMEN

Sana'a

What I learn about poetry in Yemen,
I learn at a sidewalk café off of Zubairi Street,
one of the main streets in Sana'a named
after the poet who fomented revolution with rhyme,

where I'm finishing off a plate of butterflied chicken,
the aroma of garlic and lemon marinade
mixing with the smoke fanned by a piece of cardboard box,
the grill right there on the sidewalk,

when a ragged old man tramps by looking
like a bedouin, a holy man in hard plastic shoes,
banging his walking staff on the pavement
and reciting poetry, which, even though I can't

understand, I know is poetry. Maybe the smell
of the grilled food catches his attention,
but he doesn't stop singing his poetry
as loud as his lungs will allow to the waiters, cooks,

and whoever else is listening, which I am
as I'm standing there paying my bill, and now
he's dancing—banging his staff in rhythm, stamping
a couple steps forward, a couple steps back,

BANG!—and I've got to admit that I'm feeling it too,
so I put my arms up in the air like his,
and he grasps my wrist, and suddenly
we're dancing together, the waiters smiling

and clapping as we go back and forth,
BANG! in front of the restaurant,
until the end nears, the big finish, and everyone
is standing and cheering, and I've got to

buy him lunch, I mean I've just got to, because
when was the last time I tasted poetry like this,

not just a cool mint swirl in the brain,
but a wash of chile in the marrow?

So I slam some *rials* down on the counter
for another platter of chicken and rice,
but he's got no time to sit and eat,
so the waiters bag it up for him, and off he goes

toward the city center, his bag of food
swinging from one hand, his staff in the other,
his hard shoes clopping away, my day
swinging from his neck like a medallion.

EMBRACE

Beyond my wooden shutters,
the world hums and buzzes.

The tall houses nearby
spill their secrets: a toddler

howling through bars
after a mother's cuff,

an aluminum lid
clanging onto its kettle,

an old man and an old woman
quarreling without teeth,

a girl on the roof
scowling laundry onto a clothesline.

I walk through the Old City
and the New, to the university,

where my student Marwan
tells me his dream.

I saw you, my teacher,
and you were Muslim,

he says, handing me a pamphlet
rife with misspellings.

Last night, who worried more
about my eternity than he?

Like this, I fall in love
with every pure

but imperfect intention:
every stone staircase

stacked with uneven steps,
every mud wall built

to lead me away,
every peel and pit

strewn in the fruit *souq*
because the buyer couldn't wait,

every bent key
to open a gate.

SECESSION

1.

As anti-aircraft guns begin their nightly ripping of zinc, we gather the judge's paralyzed wife in a blanket, lug her downstairs into the windowless stone hallway. Clutching the corner over her shoulder, I slip into her eye, which has surrendered to the unearthly gravity and indirect light she exists in. What fear hasn't she already known? Her husband's government fell hard. Her husband, in his seventies, took a second wife. Soon the flood started moving up her body, bathing more and more of her in a motionless blue not unlike the sky over their ancestral village. After sunset, we hunker down around her. *Minda. . .Minda. . .Minda. . .*she burbles for her Filipina nurse. Her mouth can no longer pronounce the name of her daughter, the one whispering to her now through worried fingers. She can't erase her husband's eyes, their fierce blue rings around brown, though she submerged them years ago in her memory's cistern.

2.

Heat lightning to the south could easily be artillery, the same flashing pulse miming mortars fired skyward. The news anchorman talks of traitors. The dead are never shown. Rumor has it the meat lockers in Ta'izz are full of frozen soldiers the government doesn't want to cart home. In Thamar, separatist forces leveled the electric plant before being leveled in turn. We've reached a point of not knowing, somewhere between our house and our neighbor's stone hall where we wait under blankets for dawn, recite the shortest Qur'anic *surahs*, and trust little else. Perhaps the driveway's unraked piles of crushed stone resemble the hills of Hadramaut, the volcanic rock and white dunes enemies know like the backs of unburnt hands; 30,000, maybe 80,000 hands. The lightning animates the trees in Zihra's orchard. We have never met him, nor seen what kind of fruit the lush leaves conceal, but I am certain it's sweeter than anything flesh could know.

3.

Another night snubs another day. Sunset prayer says *peace*, covering a blanket of hand-woven hair over the evening's whispers. I'm walking home beside the sewage trickling down the middle of a mud alley. Half-moons of stained glass blush from top-floor rooms, where witnesses listen to the news guaranteeing the government forces Heaven. They and their families will drink from its flooding rivers. Meanwhile, our driveway slopes away like an arched back. A boy stood there yesterday, pointing his pellet gun at the sky. A tiny ball of down perching on the TV aerial sensed the rushing metal. Children know much about war. Doubtless, death will be promised to many little boys when birds turn a deep enduring blue, the color of cobalt towers and stars flickering above hollow bones. The neighbor's children fall asleep, but their dreams crash like cymbals.

4.

One of these days a rain of rockets will unsnap the minds of street dogs. Many believers will turn palms down, revert to scripted shells, black yarn tied around ankles. I'm not afraid of what Allah wills. I try to stop boys from pegging rocks at the dogs, their minor moment of power over fangs. I'm relieved when the pack struggles out through our metal gate and flees into the street. They'll be back at night to own the boys. I've shaved my head. The reason, I say, is the heat. In the south, heads like mine are burning the arsenal al-'Anad, ripping up carpet from the luxury hotel lobby, taking what can be gripped. At home, I'm a soldier who can't satisfy his wife. Twice, I've cried like fire. Things distant ring a beauty not unlike missiles: fists buried in feather pillows, water tanks bulging near the border moments before mortars. In a distant precinct, an imam speeds up sunset. I have learned it's possible to distrust and live, to feel absolutely nothing around me.

5.

At 9:00, the same hour-long news. Continuous official rhetoric. No
sound bytes, no war footage. No analysis of strategy, trajectory,
soaring prices. No sign of killing. The president sits at a long table,
mouthing directives to military advisors. Each segment ends with a
lit Italian chandelier, the sign that the world has never had faith in
anything but firelight. My sister-in-law discovers a cockroach striding
along the living room pillows. She runs to the kitchen, comes back
pulling a thick black rubber glove onto her right hand like a surgeon.
Catching it between thumb and forefinger, she walks briskly to the
door, throws the whirling-antennae pinch into the silent twilight.
Across the courtyard, we can see the big black Xs our neighbor has
taped over her windows to prevent them from shattering. I scoff at
her feeble attempt to save until our windows fly inside.

6.

People are piling pillows, mattresses, children into pickups. They'll drive to waterless villages, set kids in concrete rooms of second cousins twice removed, and wait. No one anywhere will be relieved. Pressure from the blasts rained plaster and colored glass onto floors. Blue waterfalls of window glass surged into the street. The judge estimates his age to be 83 based on a chronology of dead relatives and tribal feuds. He knew this neighborhood before the Revolution, when Jews lived in the sunken houses. I ride with him and his grandson to the explosion site. The soldier at the roadblock kisses his hand, lets only him pass through the rubble. Fifteen minutes later, he returns, drops into my hand a mangled metal clot. It is strong, light, a piece of the missile housing. The night it fell, dozens of dogs in the empty lot opposite the presidential palace bayed in a way I'd never heard before, a way that made women lock their children indoors, slip buckets outside to catch the impending storm.

7.

Missiles in the Eid of Sacrifice. Few risk praying sunset prayer at
mosques near the Republican Palace. However, on Hadda Street
the ice cream shop is full of customers. Crowding over the cold
cases, veiled girls wait boldly for Syrian pistachio. Young kids shout
for brown paper pouches of potato chips, shakers of salt and
cayenne. From the rolled-down windows of Land Cruisers, sons
of the rich blare Michael Jackson, hope their friends see them
smooth as new bullets, bold in the face of missiles. They'll roar
down the emptied streets, blurring the blue doors to perfection. All
their favorite shops remain open till curfew: music, burgers, videos,
mango juice. In the market, what I want is out of stock. No relief
from the monotony I've discovered in my mortal home. In a small
mosque, old men read *Surat Yaseen* in unison for those whose homes
Monday's Scud exploded over them, whose belongings were
snatched out of the piles of glass, broken bricks, and bodies, by
looters.

8.

Month of honey, month of missiles. On the way to the neighbor's
hallway, I stoop through my doorway and swim in the clean, purple
sky. The Big Dipper has been upturned for months, no sign of
dissipation. On Channel One, a man pried from the wreckage praises
Allah from a bed in al-Salaam Hospital. Under one mud building,
25 bludgeoned. The whitecaps of your nightgown roll toward the
warm beach of night. I make plans by praying. Plans with you and
falling water, flattened trees, the earth of a different brown country.
Whatever manner of flesh will rekindle our blackened bones, Allah
can raise it above the pounding, cover it with the coolest mist.

THE GOLD SHOP OF BA-'ALI

al-Mukalla

They step up to the display case, an old father,
his wife, and a daughter newly engaged.
They have come from a hot village.
The father removes an old kerchief from his pocket,
unwraps baubles to trade as they shop

for their daughter's bridal gold. In *Souq al-Nisa'*,
serious buyers come here first. *We've been here
too long to need a sign*, whispers a son of Ba-'Ali.
From the back room floats forward
the saline odor of a small, desiccated shark.

Perhaps tomorrow, after soaking overnight
in sweet water and stewing since dawn
with tomato and onion, it'll become breakfast.
A thin son of Ba-'Ali leaving the back room
sulks through the shop, greeting no one.

After sunset, he'll head down to the waterfront,
to the teashop where young men play chess,
swatting their timers fiercely after each move.
Two days of traveling away, my wife
takes care of our newborn twins at home.

Bearing my glaringly foreign surname,
they cling to life despite odds impossible
had I not believed in higher hands.
Yet I flew away from them, away from my wife,
away from this republic for something else.

But in al-Hudaydah, the sand whipped around fighter planes
junked behind the runway. Over the mountains,
I was jostled from air pocket to pocket like a nervous coin.
At Aden airport, an Egyptian teacher perched on his luggage
for the long layover could only curse. *They are dogs,*

all of them, he said, cigarette smoke knifing out
between his teeth. It was then I knew I had to stay.
I walked out of the airport and called my nearest friend,
a son of Ba-'Ali. A crammed taxi across the desert
for a day, and I arrived. The oldest son of Ba-'Ali

opens the safe, shows me a tray of a jewelry.
His father's eye squints tighter around the jeweler's eyeglass.
When we were introduced, each son shook my hand
and kissed his father's. I imagine Ba-'Ali's bride
slipping her fingers into a glove of gold mail

and thick coins the first time, the weight a promise asks.
Now I am holding her private gold! On another tray,
old trinkets wait to be melted down and reborn
as whatever is the current rage in Bahrain.
There, I find something to resurrect, something

to grace my wife: big crescent earrings with bangles
dangling in the wane. A son of Ba-'Ali bathes my choice
in solvent till it glows. Soon, I will return home
with bright Indian shawls and gold. When I give her the gold,
she will thank me politely and put it away, forever.

RAINY SEASON

I try not to look foolish.
But as I'm trundling the big key
in the wooden lock, a chameleon twitches in
between the hinges. It skitters across the ceiling,
into the folds of the distant bedroom where
our premature twins sleep under a gauze tent.
I spend the night watching pockets of air
empty and fill inside their chests.

Babies born in the eighth month never survive,
old women tell my wife. But ours
have now crawled to the back door,
where they are clucking their tongues,
coaxing stray cats over walls crowned with broken glass.
The cats sit just out of reach, in tall weeds,
waiting for our daily chicken-intestine charity.
I thank Allah for intestines and tongues.

The only healthy tree in the garden is a sour
pomegranate, whose scarlet coronets blat and blare.
Several months from now, the retired judge
living upstairs will bid me present the fruit
from the highest branches to him. I'll teeter
to reach each gorgeous blushing orb, yank,
but the jeweled chambers will have been gutted
by churlish birds. Still, I'll deliver them.

In a few hours, brown torrents will flood the city again.
The market will be cleansed of people, date stones,
egg shells and feathers, banana peels, goat hooves,
all washed into an alluvial plain. As I see it, rain
is a solvent. That's how weeds in empty lots
grow inches overnight, why I spend so much time
in my window the morning before today's rain,
the morning after yesterday's.

PRAYING BESIDE THE *MUJAHED*

He and his Kalashnikov have known
more reasons to pray than the *imam* leading us,
who grinds out the same verses as if Allah
were a big deaf ear.

His flak jacket smells of terraced mountains
before the rain, fields of wind rumbling past
as he leans over the cab of a pickup plummeting
into the world's last valley.

After surveying the dead, the brothers
who died with peaceful smiles, he buried them
in gardens of rubble. Soon, red blossoms unfolded
with the promise of musk.

Were I to turn my head to the left, I could gaze
deep into the dark eye of the Kalashnikov.
Never think that a trigger tripped, a skull separated
onto plush carpet, is an accident, for destiny

allows no accidents. After the prayer, we'll say *peace*.
His hand will shake mine with vigor. Until then,
closing my eyes, all I can see are onions, glorious
and sweet, thundering in the damp loam of Heaven.

SYRIA

FIRST BREAKFAST

Sultan Hotel, Damascus, 2005

Outside of our room burdened with luggage,
through the hallway bannered with kilim,
we bid good morning to Mr. Muhammad,
the receptionist finishing his shift, and drift
to a corner table in the dining room,

where my daughter opens the sticky menu
like a bilingual holy book,
both tongues of which she can speak.
She is rapt in the offerings.
But before she can choose,

an arthritic waiter shuffles over
with a basket of hard rolls.
On a second trip he brings
a saucer puddled with jam,
pats of butter cramped in foil,

a teapot that clanks. The world
gave her the illusion of choice
then whisked it away. On the scale
of her eyes, she is already weighing
deception versus truth, the ethics

of false promises. I whisper,
There is nothing else in their kitchen.
Meanwhile, people we will never know
have occupied tables near us,
their cigarettes bluing the air.

In the honesty of my wife's lap,
my daughter begins to cry.
I swallow my bread, listening
to the gentlest fountain in all of Damascus
burbling on this whitest of mornings.

LETTER FROM DAMASCUS

to Mark Vinz

The snowstorm that hit the Midwest after I left
made the local news here. When people ask
which state I'm from, Florida or New York,
I tell them the one hit by the blizzard, the one
they'd never heard of before. In Damascus,
January is more like a Minnesota spring: rainy,
with a chill that can seize the joints. Beyond weather,
the air is full of religion. Strange to say that
about a country run by a dictator's son
and his party, but the facts are on the ground.
When Paul of Tarsus rode into town on a donkey,
he was struck down on the street called Straight
just a few blocks from my hotel. Now the street,
narrow enough to be paralyzed by a couple of cars,
is festooned with Islamic banners, bustling
with shoppers buying spices, sweets, sensible clothes.
Holy places remain holy, no matter who's in control.
Think Jerusalem. Think the Black Hills. Or here,
where an Aramaean shrine turned Roman temple turned
cathedral turned mosque. Maybe the same is true
of people: the good stay good and no matter what
they are doomed. In the Umayyad Mosque is a shrine
containing the head of John the Baptist, and it is said
that when Jesus returns, he'll touch down near
the southeastern minaret. Even the previous Pope
stopped during his Mideastern tour to gaze skyward.
Meanwhile, the Prophet Muhammad's companions
and grandchildren are enshrined nearby as if
they were neighbors. Syrians revere graves.
Perhaps that's what happens when one lives
atop so much time. You can't help but ponder
who came before, how we arrived, why we're given
something small but strong inside, something
so strong that words can't help but follow.

LETTER FROM DAMASCUS

to Thom Tammaro

North of Mt. Qassioun, where I'll soon go,
it's snowing. Big, gloppy plops of snow
perch atop mountain scrub and rocks like a million
frog-princes waiting to be freed from their curses.
No one dares criticize the regime. Hung
in every room, the young president's face presides,
trying hard to look determined and visionary.
Meanwhile in the National Museum, each chamber
contains an entire civilization: Ugaritic, Eblaic,
Sumerian, Seleucid, Roman, Umayyad, Ottoman.
As I walked through millennia, an old woman followed,
staring at me from the shadows, reciting something
in a tongue incomprehensible to me or my guide.
She wouldn't stop. But I could tell it was poetry
from the meter and rhyme, hers the only voice
flashing through the holy halls of history,
the yawp of a lone, demented life among the dead.
On the streets, people dress with flair:
professional men in suits, Brylcreem,
and glossy shoes; women coiffed, mascara-ed,
and highly heeled. I want to say *so Italian*.
I'm certain that Damascus, like other cities I've seen
on the Mediterranean's south and east,
would gently lower her wing for you.
I was watching Al Jazeera on the hotel lobby TV,
and in the corner of the screen a man signed for the deaf,
speaking Arabic with hands, shoulders, head,
his whole body giving birth to loud but silent
meaning. Maybe someday destiny will send us
traveling together far from our Midwestern home,
somewhere to capture succinctly the flavor
of pistachio, the treasure of olive, what words
can still do after having already, surely, done everything.

FESTIVAL OF SACRIFICE

Homs

The concierge hasn't heard
of any celebration
other than the show advertised

on the lobby poster: a belly dancer
performing in the cabaret,
her sloe eyes pouting in blue shadow,

her bosoms and blue tassels
defying gravity. *She must be
from a village*, my wife whispers.

Even if there were somewhere to go,
we'd need coins for cab fare,
but the cashier says she can't make change.

I blow big bills on room service
and reluctant tips. My wife and I
take turns watching our sick son

while the other goes out for air.
My turn outside, I take along
my daughter, who's all dressed up

in a frilly pink holiday dress, tights,
and sequined shoes, her long hair
tamed by combs and bows.

The sun shines for its hour.
My daughter and I stroll hand in hand.
The streets are empty except

for patriarchs leaving their gates
with armfuls of aromatic grass
to set upon loved ones' graves.

We walk past the statue of
the former president, his arms
frozen in a gesture that says,

Behold what I have done.
And I do behold, I really think I do.
Yesterday on my walk, for instance,

I beheld a park. Yes, here it is now,
inside this stone gate—
the Garden of Abdulbasit Al-Sufi,

whom I haven't heard of before,
but that's no surprise.
All of his seesaws are broken

except one, so my daughter celebrates
the one by perching on its rusted seat.
On the other end I lever her up,

holding her there until she pleads for release,
my distressed damsel. On the sidewalk,
three boys prance their bejeweled ponies

back and forth while a few waifs dangle
from chain swings, watching us try
to make the most out of the moment.

HUSSAM'S HEART

al-Wa'r

My flat smells stale, so I go ask Hussam,
the young neighborhood grocer, if he sells incense,
a shard to crumble over my censer's coals.
He raises his eyebrows once, slowly, which in Syrian

means no. But then he pauses. He stands
on a plastic chair and, digging behind the stacked perfumes,
he finds what he's looking for. He brings it to the counter
and sets it in front of me: a small Damascene box,

a geometry of wood and mother-of-pearl.
Hinging open the lid, he reveals a red velvet lining
cushioning a chunk of incense pressed into the shape of a heart,
beside it a tiny silver hammer. The heart is his, he says,

meaning it's not for sale. *Hadiya hay min habibti,*
this gift was from his beloved. *Habibti*—the feminine grammar
even the most tear-drenched love songs can't bring themselves
to utter, the faint pulse of a concluded tragedy:

she was a bedouin in his eastern town,
they were in love but their fathers refused the matrimony.
They were so in love they even contemplated running away.
But without family, to whom would they run?

So that was it, the period ending the book.
She sent him this box, this fragrant heart for him to break, burn,
and remember. He cracks off a lobe. *Khuth,* he tells me, take it,
and holds it out to me, both of us waiting for what comes next.

GYPSY CAMP, AL-WA'R

for Fathia

After the smocked children of the neighborhood
yawn to school and their parents frown to work,

we stroll past the abandoned apartment blocks
to the park flourishing with weeds:

poppies offering up cup after cup, pansies flashing
like doubloons, thistles bristling armored purple.

But you are more interested in what lies behind
in the hovels of tarp and branches, where people live

whom our neighbors curse with one small word.
Their menfolk amble home after dark with empty pails.

Their womenfolk dry scavenged potato peels on the sidewalk
to feed their goats. No one is friendlier to dogs.

You pretend to inspect more weeds, drifting closer,
closer to a tarp-and-branch hovel until dogs bark,

goats spook, and from the door-flap an old woman
emerges, gripping a twig broom. When she sees you,

she smiles, invites you inside, while I wait
on a cement park bench until you return

through the thorns and blooms, a smile like hers,
your mind full of tales that must be true.

PRISON BEADS

A bouquet of blue flowers that never wilts,

a stand for the Qur'an,

Arabic script knotted into geometry,

brightly colored birds flitting

among green garlands,

an almond eye crying turquoise tears,

clusters of grapes blushing on the vine,

prayer beads, each bearing one of God's ninety-nine names—

over and over I marvel

at what hangs from suction cups

stuck inside the windshields of taxi vans:

as if I am riding in a boat

on a river in Paradise.

I ask, *Where can I buy these?*

But every driver says the same.

They are not in the market.

They are not for sale.

THE BUS FROM HOMS TO DAMASCUS

backs out of the grimy Karnak Station
as soon as the barker boy shouting
Al-Sham Al-Sham Al-Sham
fills the seats. I've learned he means

Damascus, the capital which so many
of us need. I find a window seat
above the back wheel, in the shade,
and we begin winding through the dusty

precincts of Homs, picking up extras
who are willing to sit on the floor.
Barring engine trouble, the trip
means two hours in a cramped seat

near a window that would be inconsiderate
of me to open. Outside of town,
we split the grove of wispy pines
permanently leaned east by a wind

whose memory blows across the plain
though today there's not even a breeze.
In the desert, an old man has the bus pull over
next to a stick stuck into the ground,

where his family stands waiting in the heat,
their own bodies giving the world
its only shade. We drive on
until the bus stops again, this time

for a young couple to board. Seats are changed
so the couple can sit together:
wife gripping a blanket-wrapped infant
enters the window seat; husband buffers

her immodest bend from public gaze
and pulls the window curtain shut.
He has demonstrated gallant responsibility.
To pass the time, the barker boy

pushes a grainy cassette into the VCR.
It's *Total Recall*, Schwarzenegger on Mars
trying to know his own mind. Everybody in the bus
seems ragged from the heat, from the need

to go to the capital for work, money,
papers stamped and signed by the right ministries.
And then Schwarzenegger reaches deep
into his own sinuses with a pair of pliers

to yank out the sensor implanted there
before his mind was erased. Perhaps this
is the best my country can offer: science fiction
with hero, girl, and villain. Hero wants

to save the tired, the poor, the huddled
irradiated masses yearning to breathe free.
It's hard to tell which girl is his enemy,
a double agent, and which is his lover.

I wonder if Syrians wonder the same about me,
but Schwarzenegger, girl, and villain
have just been sucked by the hyper-gravity
out of the portal and rolled down the Martian dunes,

their eyes bulging out of their sockets
from the pressure. The red landscape
resembles the mountains outside my window
through which we're now winding,

some villages isolated for so long
they still speak Aramaic, the language of Christ.
To pass the time, I've taken to *tasbeeh*,
clacking *Glory to Allah*, *Praise to Allah*,

Allah is Great, on my green plastic prayer beads
until we pull into the chaos of al-'Abbasiyeen Station,
where the most important things are instinct
and another bus to make it back to the crust.

LETTER FROM HAMA

to Sameer

In a tea shack on the outskirts of Sana'a, Yemen,
you explained the fifteen Arabic poetic meters,
pounding out a *taweel* on the metal table—
ba-bang-bang ba-bang-bang–during a blackout.
The candle on the table trembled. The tea guy,
behind his battered pots, dreamed of home.
It must've been the same meter your wife
made with her high heels through the hallway,
past the row of her own cryptic oil paintings,
and out the door, forever, the same meter
as the whey dripping from yoghurt
balled in cheesecloth over the sink,
amplified a thousand times. A decade later,
I'm walking around rubble in Hama, your hometown.
The landscape of old homes and narrow alleys,
leveled by your former president,
has been repainted with riverside cafés and gardens,
so much beauty masking so much blood.
The wooden waterwheels continue their chronic
creaking and groaning as if nothing ever ended.
The government has made it clear: a university
will never be built here, so the youth must commute
to the one an hour away, where I teach,
where they are among my best students.
Perhaps the only true place for poets is
in a foreign land, on the outskirts of town,
thinking about the home to which
complete return is impossible, about the void
into which the people we love disappear,
where the sound of a fist goes after banging.

SACRIFICE

for Sameer

No better place to slaughter than your bathroom.
After *Eid* prayer, you rented the young butcher,
knives and all. Now, his skirted knee is poised
on the sheep's shoulder. *Bismillah*, and the blade
will dissolve flesh. As he cups the sheep's muzzle,
exposing its long, soft neck, for just a moment
I don't believe in death.

But the lurch of blood comes, the spastic
hooves skittering to silence. Blood coils, lugubrious,
across the pink-tiled floor, fading down the drain.
I remember your stories about Hama, your hometown
until your president shredded it like a stomach:
50,000 citizens disappeared into the tan earth.
I hear so little news.

He works methodically, dismantling the legs,
spreading the rib cage open to reveal organs
dangling like glass ornaments. He rinses the intestines,
twines them between his square hands.
Your own son is a knife: *al-Muhannad*,
the Prophet's strong Indian sword. When he grows up,
what will he strike? How will he sound?

During nightly power outages, you offer food:
cold *kibbeh*, salad flashing with onion and mint,
Turkish coffee. You stand a candle into the drop
of wax on the tabletop, echo 'Antara and Poe
through your apartment's barren corridor.
When your wife left through it, her heels cursed in code.
For such reasons, I never memorize poems.

The butcher boy gets paid in brains and hide.
We divvy the meat: one sack for neighbors,
one for the poor whose knuckles test
the patience of doors, and one for ourselves.
What we give we'll regain, we believe.
Your son will visit. You will remarry.
Every severed nerve will explain.

ORIENTAL BATMAN

an antique shop in Hama

In the twilight over al-Hamra Zone, where the grotesquerie
of doctored concrete festers under viny bougainvillea,
I see you fluttering down the palm-lined boulevard

past fountains sizzling with colored lights. You sink
your pin-fangs into the fleshy yellow *acadinia* nubs,
sucking their nectar, the fuzz of your muzzle glistening,

the meal so ethereal, so dazzling that, by the next morning,
after the fountains have fizzled into snarls of wet wire,
you sprawl on the marble esplanade, spread-membraned drunk.

No one notices, not even the blue-smocked children
shouting by rote their lesson in the nearby school,
the same darlings who, at noon, pelt the beaded nag

that pulls the fuel-oil cart just to see her withers
shiver like magic slats. Still I cannot comprehend power.
When the government slices open the oyster

of your city and swallows it, pearl and all,
the waterwheels on the Stubborn River keep groaning.
I know you've had some close calls. And when

you finally call it quits, you open this shop, stock it
to the rafters with debris: shoeboxes of postcards
written in the scripts of Parisian women, the tasseled

camel bags of bedouins from the Eastern Desert,
amulets from Byzantium. Whenever I visit,
your shop is locked. But perhaps, as your neighbors

recite their night prayers, you'll flap back for a sip,
the casks of the waterwheel gargling like larynxes,
scooping, spilling, splashing, your name, your name.

MY BEAUTIFUL SYRIAN STUDENTS
PRACTICE THEIR CURSIVE

a found poem, gleaned from homework at the university in Homs

I have brown eyes.

    She is like the moon.

You are invited to my birthday party.

       My hair is as smooth as silk.

    Were I you, I would be more patient.

I am starving.

    I want a candle-light dinner.

       I ache all over.

Call again if it is urgent.

    I will meet you in my spare time.

       Sooner or later, justice will be done.

    Let the rain come down and wash away my tears.

The purpose of teaching has become different from what it used to be.

       Did he jump or was he pushed?

WHAT I LEARN ABOUT POETRY IN SYRIA

Homs

What I learn about poetry in Syria, I learn in a mosque.
As soon as the congregational prayer ends,

he's at my elbow, a student of mine from the university.
He wants to introduce me to the *imam* who just gave the sermon.

I can't say no. So he leads me through the crowd of lingering men
to the prayer niche up front. "The imam is my friend," he says,

and opens a secret door. There, in a long room lined with chairs
sits the *imam*, surrounded by his retinue waiting for extra inspiration.

Room is made for me on the highest couch next to the imam, while
my student kneels at my feet, ready to translate in case my Arabic fails.

I repeat my oft-repeated sentences of self-introduction:
I am an American professor teaching English at the university,

I am an exchange professor teaching here for only one semester,
I embraced Islam 15 years ago in Yemen, I like Syria generally,

though of course there are good people as well as bad people everywhere,
and I write poetry. The imam's eyes widen: "Ah, you are a poet!"

His retinue sighs with delight. "That's wonderful!" he smiles.
"Let us hear one of your poems!"

I feel my face getting warm. "I'm sorry," I say, "but I haven't memorized
any of my poems, and I don't have any of my poems written down with me."

Throughout the room, foreheads squinch in puzzlement. I try to explain.
"Poetry in America is different from poetry in the Middle East," I begin.

"In America, poets depend on written-down poems. The writing is important,
the recitation, less so. American poets usually read their poems;

they don't usually memorize them and recite them as you do here."
Hmm. . .Aahhh. . . the crowd buzzes, still puzzled, but polite.

The *imam* intervenes graciously, sparing me from the silence.
"Well, if not one of your own poems, perhaps you can

recite a poem by someone else, perhaps a famous English poet,
and then your student can translate it for us?"

I count the years that have passed since my last doctoral comprehensive exam.
Six. At that time, I memorized a Shakespearean sonnet to illustrate the parts.

Hard as I try, I can't conjure it. It evaporated long ago. There is nothing,
absolutely nothing I can provide this hungry audience,

not a single poem for the *imam*, my poor student, or even myself.
The retinue must think me a charlatan. What kind of poet

doesn't remember even one poem of his own? This time,
my student speaks, offering a poem by Donne that he memorized

in another professor's class, then translating it into Arabic.
*Hmmm. . . Ahhhh. . .*the room coos. The *imam* turns again to me:

"Anyway, we are most happy to meet you, our dear respected
Muslim brother from America." As he begins his lesson to his followers,

I excuse myself to meet my wife and daughter outside.
Everyone smiles.

CONSPIRACY THEORY

I'm sitting in the mosque after prayer when Dr. Jihad wants to show me something before returning to surgery. *Have you seen this before?* he asks, pulling out a $20 bill. Have I seen a $20 bill before? He can't mean that, even though, honestly, I don't see them very much since I began using my credit card for everything, even gum. Before I can ask what he means, he starts folding it, first in half horizontally then at odd angles, until he hands me the V-shaped origami. On the backside of the bill, what was the bucolic White House now stands on end, the shrubbed landscape turned out to the sides, the sleepy windows rising in story upon story of glass and steel. It's the Twin Towers! And near the top floors, what were stately trees framing the President's residence now burst into flames, smoke like torches. *Why is THIS on the American money?* Dr. Jihad asks, shaking the proof in front of me. Then, unfolding it, accordioning it in another direction, he turns the 20 and the UNITED STATES OF AMERICA into O-S-A-M-A. *How can the American Government NOT know this is on their money? A coincidence? Come on,* he says. *Where are the black boxes? Where is the gold?*

THE GOLDEN HAMSTER

Every pet golden hamster in the world can be traced
back to a pair of field hamsters captured in Syria.

In the Eastern Desert, he squats
in the shade cast by his overheated roadster,
his guide toiling under the engine bonnet.

He sits in a bedouin's black hair tent,
the *qahweh* dribbling again from the beak
of a brass pot into a thimble-cup.

He lies on a sheepskin, worrying about
the roadster, how much longer it will take to fix,
the track back to Jerusalem.

In the darkness, he hears his guide and the bedouin
murmur *fajr* prayer in hushed tones.
He tries to return to sleep,

but the world begins
chattering with the news
of what he must take with him.

AL-MUTANABBI'S DOOR

with versions of Arberry's translations

Because of his prodigious poetic skill and ego, Abu al-Tayyib Ahmad ibn al-Husayn al-Kindi became known as al-Mutanabbi, "the one claiming to be a prophet." His greatest poetic output occurred during his nine years as court poet for Sayf al-Dawla, the Emir of Aleppo, in the mid-10th century.

Easter 2005: whenever my family and I enter an Aleppine hotel, the receptionist raises his eyebrows once, Syrian body language for no. Though I'm a Muslim, I'm thinking of the Bible story about Jesus' birth in Bethlehem—in Arabic, *Bayt Lahm*—"House of Meat."

> *The worst land is a place where there's no friend.*
> *The worst thing a person can earn is dishonor.*

Aleppo—in Arabic, *Halab*—means "milk," the place, it is said, where the Prophet Abraham stopped to milk his cow on the way from Mesopotamia to a land that would become holy after he arrived.

> *Where have you decided to go, gallant hero?*
> *We are the plants on the hills, and you are the clouds.*

At *Funduq al-Gawaher*—"Hotel of Jewels"—we take the only room left. The sink slobbers onto the floor. The bedspreads bear their blotches. I lean against the tapestry, smashing hidden mosquitoes between the Armenian letters and the pink wall.

> *I've reached the point that when arrows strike me,*
> *the tips break against each other.*

In the Great Mosque, where people hang combination locks onto the grating around Prophet Zakariah's tomb, I ask the old custodian, *Ayna bayt al-Mutanabbi*, "Where is al-Mutanabbi's house?" His hand angles and jabs the air.

> *When I behold you, my eyes are too dazzled.*
> *When I praise you, my tongue too bewildered.*

Corridors of shops selling inlaid wooden boxes and red tapestries. Corridors of olives, almonds, and *fustuq halabi*—pistachios. A soap-seller unfolds his jackknife, pulls the blade through a brown bar of olive-oil soap, revealing a jade core, till the blade presses against his thumb.

> *Bless you for the rain that you are, as if our skin*
> *sprouts brocade, embroidered silk, and fine robes.*

From a cart, a vendor sells tumblers of *soos*—bitter black tonic made from licorice root. It's said a *Halabi* merchant can sell anything, even the stiff hide of a donkey.

> *He is the sea—dive into it for pearls when it's still,*
> *but beware when it's foaming.*

For nearly a decade, al-Mutanabbi praised Emir Sayf al-Daula. Or was he praising himself?

> *He knows the secrets of all religions and languages.*
> *His thoughts put people and books to shame.*

Ayna bayt al-Mutanabbi? I ask a young man walking alone. He pauses to explain, then beckons I follow him. More alleys. He stops before a door.

> *The horse, the night, and the desert know me,*
> *and the sword and the spear, and the paper and the pen.*

Heavy. Wooden. Plain. Painted orange and brown. A small plaque beside it says *Mu'assasat al-Nisaa'*—"Women's Foundation."

> *Everything Allah has created and hasn't created*
> *means as little to me as a single hair on my head.*

I knock. No one opens. A passerby says it's closed, and shrugs away. "For the day? The weekend? Forever? Until when?"

What is time but a reciter of my lines—
when I compose a poem, time recites it.

In the emir's court, al-Mutanabbi's chief poetic rival was Abu Firas al-Hamdani, the emir's own cousin. When the blood ties tightened around him, al-Mutanabbi fled to Egypt.

When you see the lion bare its fangs,
do not suppose it's smiling.

Six years after leaving *Halab*, I'm watching the Arab Spring blossom on Al Jazeera TV. Hesitant demonstrators gather in alleys. A soldier's rifle cracks, scattering them like mice.

Can a hunk of meat on a butcher's block reign
when swords are thirsty and birds are hungry?

Two years after the Arab Spring, opposition and government forces battle for each street. Breaking news: the minaret of the Great Mosque in *Halab* has been toppled by government artillery.

In the twilight, helicopters dangle barrels of explosives over neighborhoods.

Despite its bold edge, you'll find that the sword
in the hand of a coward becomes a coward itself.

Ten years have passed since I spent one day of my life in *Halab*.

I'm nothing but an arrow in the air, returning
because I didn't find anything there to grasp.

That day I knocked on al-Mutanabbi's door. Or maybe it was just a door.

THE BIRDS OF AL-MERJEH SQUARE

Damascus

On a sidewalk table in front of the Star of the East Hotel,

two cages sit side by side, an old gray parrot perched in each.

A boy darting past rattles an empty soda can across the cages.

Another boy hovers, pressing through the bars a grape.

In the afternoon, as we stroll, young moneychangers

on the street corners coo *change*, *change*. Question, or command?

A traffic soldier blusters away a flock of taxis stopping for fares.

In the square, pink bushes roost within their marble pen

while the green-plumed river struts down its cement trench.

Overhead, swallows screech and dart among the façades.

A man in a window hails seed onto a steel canopy for pigeons.

In the morning, leaving the hotel forever, we find

one cage empty, while on the other, with door agape,

the last parrot is climbing, beak and claw, toward the air.

NIGERIA

THE MESSIAH OF KOGI STATE

1.

Lokoja

The longer you wait for someone, the more important he must be. In the gubernatorial hall, my colleagues and I wait an hour for the Cabinet to arrive. Another hour for the Governor, who is actually governor, prince, and millionaire in one person, a Nigerian power trinity. *Your Excellency, Messiah of Kogi State, I crave your indulgence to intimate*, the court emcee begins, and I know there is no escape. I am marooned for the duration. Protocol demands a strict order of introduction, starting with the least important, growing longer and longer until only the governor himself remains. At the reception, a Cabinet minister pumps my hand. *We are so grateful that you white professors have come*; he smiles into the reddening mask of my face. The ghost of empire is everywhere, even in the bread. White, fine-crumbed, sweet as wedding cake, the square slices float to our table on a silver platter with tea at every breakfast. Until the governor bids his aide fetch us for a function, we are captives, a harem of child brides starved for love. Flanked by armed MOPOL guards, we are paraded in public, then returned to the confines of the palace. Once, I slip outside to watch a sunset. Right before my eyes, the sky ripens like warm fruit. Then, something starts eating it—a silent horde of flying foxes winging toward their nocturnal feeding, an exquisite plague. Late at night I lie in my private chamber and watch African satellite TV: South African CNN, a soap opera with HIV-positive lovers in a bantustan, a cop show in Afrikaans. On the Nigerian channel, the breaking news is an heiress's birthday party in Lagos, music courtesy of King Sunny Adé and his African Beats. Usually I fall asleep watching; it drowns out the sounds from the adjacent room, where Mr. Innocent Chukwu sits like a chieftain fingering his beaded cane until a servant girl taps on his door. And when I wake hours later, the television's white noise sounds like a waterfall, like hundreds of bullfrogs croaking *one, one, one*, in hoarse unison, over and over.

2.

Lokoja

In the gubernatorial auditorium, the official state dancers dance for us, a command performance. In front-row seats we sit with napkins of savories and sweets, bottles of Coke balanced on our laps. Dancers appear in tribal costumes, stamping and thrusting toward us, below the vigilant gaze of the Governor and the President whose portraits hang on the wall. The drums surrender to weeping strings, calling a single figure onto the stage. Wearing a red Hydra mask, yellow bodice and bustle, she floats like a new lover, sure and unsure, beckoning and fleeing, an orchid with only hours to live. When young women dance, the world turns voyeur, remembering what was, what could have been so long, long ago. Only near the end do her ankles reveal their poison: beneath the costume is a man. My eyes ask to be blind. I am ashamed of being seduced. I want to forget the evening. I want to forget that I am in Kogi not for instruction but for show. I am here to stand out, a white thumbs-up for the Governor's reelection. Like a Shakespearean Capulet, I bite it. After the performance, I ask about the accompanying lyrics. All were political jingles praising the Governor. My ears ask to be deaf. Backstage, the dancers ask, *Can we study in America?* I want to tell all of them *Yes, yes, you will be loved.* Their questions, their smiles seem so naïve. Are they real? Addresses scrawled on scraps of paper are handed to me. One dancer gives me the address of an uncle in Philadelphia written on pharmaceutical stationery: Viagra. The Governor invites us to his private chamber. His stewards bubble the glasses of my female colleagues with champagne. He flirts with them as the goblets clink and fizz. I wonder about motives. Perhaps everything is deliberate. Perhaps everyone has a reason. I wonder what mine is.

3.

Idah

The center of town is a man, the leader of an entire tribe. Like a queen bee in the core of a hive, the Atta Igala is being courted by our host, the Governor. On display, we are sacs of pollen, the living, bulbous proof of his Western connections. With the Atta's endorsement, he could carry the entire tribe. *Ride On!* the buttons and banners say, showing the Governor and the Atta stepping arm in arm into the future. In the Atta's stadium, we sit for hours, never moving from our reserved row of white plastic chairs on the viewing platform. Pressed within tiers of local dignitaries, there is no room to move as we listen to speeches in Igala, watch the field of subjects become a crashing sea. Never have I seen so many people so tightly squeezed. Troupes of masqueraders cut their way through the limbs of humanity. Smoke curls out of a masked head. Coins fly toward another, bribes against bad fortune. A third figure resembles a giant cloth tube limp on a stretcher. But as drums beckon, the tube comes to life, climbing and whipping the throng before settling again on the stretcher, an airless balloon. I try to dissect the illusion; no room for a man, not even a boy, inside. What can possess these costumes other than ancestral spirits? The dignitary sitting beside me calls it old superstition. But I see the crowd cleave in fear of Smoking Head as he stamps toward them. And as my female colleague points her camera, ladies in the row behind us shout, *No! No! Do not photograph this one! You will be barren!* My colleague puts her camera into her lap. Today, His Excellency The Governor, the Messiah of Kogi State, receives another title: from this day forward, he will also be called Living Legend. I close my eyes. I don't know how many more claustrophobic hours pass. But finally my female colleague breaks down. *I'm sorry, I'm sorry, I just can't take it anymore,* she says through convulsive sobs. To the Governor and the Atta, the excuse is acceptable: women are weak. I thank her for her weakness while a Nigerian Boy Scout blazes us a trail through the bodies, away.

4.

Anyigba

I've seen the name for this village spelled different ways, though
when locals pronounce it, it sounds like none. The colonial alphabet
tries to hold captive the local sounds, but it can't. Something remains
uncaptured, undefined in the mouth. The university halls hide inside
fields of oil palm, cassava, maize, and yam vines tendrilling up
bamboo stakes. The guesthouse in which I am lodging is more
luxurious than all of the houses I've seen except the Vice-
Chancellor's. We never run out of water for long; when it's gone, a
tanker truck is summoned to fill the roof cistern. And when the
generator sputters on its last sip of petrol, a servant fetches more
in a glass jar. The Faculty Club nearby houses a swimming pool,
but the puddle of water above the plugged drain blooms emerald
with algae. I sit in a plastic chair sipping a tepid bottle of Coke,
watching two lean puppies frolic on the dance floor. A week later, I
see one of them again, upside-down on the shoulder of a young
man walking down the road, its eyes masked tightly by a hand. I
don't believe he wants to eat the dog. He probably bought it as a
watchdog and doesn't want it wandering back. The roads are lined
with mango trees, which I identify not by corpulent globes dripping
from branches but by the fuzzy elliptical discs strewn on the sand.
Wrong season. During my afternoon walks, I look for animals, a
scurry across the road, a rustle within a thicket, until a professor
tells me: *We've eaten them all*. An empty belly doesn't see beauty. All
I've spotted are white-headed crows picking refuse, pink-headed
lizards twitching for mates, and a dark bird that, while winging away,
reveals an arc of brilliant turquoise. Secrets reveal themselves in
startling ways, answers to questions I haven't asked.

5.

Anyigba

On the table is a feast: fufu, draw soup, fried *ilu* fish, fried chicken, jolof rice, garden eggs, and the *pièce de résistance*, bush meat—a large rodent whose paws have been simmered into fists. It is called grass-cutter. It tastes like wood smoke, singed fur, rock salt, beef jerky. The meal took six cooks all day to prepare. Margaret, the chef-matron, commanded the stewards to go to the market for supplies. They returned with enough sagging plastic bags to fill a taxi, including the trunk, in which a small flock of confused, sinewy chickens bound together at the legs waited next to a dead grass-cutter lashed to a stick. A cooking fire popped in the yard. Yams were peeled, boiled, pounded, and steamed into fufu. As the stewards slowly serve, I practice my Igala: *nagu, nagu*, I say constantly, thank you, thank you. I cannot say it enough. After tea, plastic mugs brim with palm wine. Thus begins the slow slouch over the arms of the white leather couches. Except Professor Rems. Eyes afire, hair smoldering, fanned by each refill, he chatters like a ventriloquist's possessed dummy. He recites the addresses and phone numbers of his student apartments in America decades ago. He recites the lyrics of Buddy Holly songs— "Words of Love," "Peggy Sue," "Oh Boy"—no melody, just the lyrics at lightning speed. He recites all of the cities along Route 66 before slumping asleep against his colleague. Rems, who returned to his homeland with American degrees, who taught two generations of citizens, who will retire after final exams, was robbed at gunpoint while driving last week. The thief stole his books, his chalk, even his shoes. Rems, ancient knight standing barefoot with his hands up, watched his Peugeot swerve down the forest road without him toward the setting sun, the thief behind the wheel barely old enough to reach the pedals.

6.

Abuja

In the national capital, my colleagues and I hurry up and wait—
hurry up to board the bus, wait for Pastor, the Governor's aide, to
tell us when to get out. He parades us from government ministry
to media outlet. We shake hands, smile, and leave. Patience burns
off layer by layer, like skin. Our MOPOL guards haven't been fed.
They ask Pastor for half an hour to take their lunch. *Do you know
who I am?* Pastor shouts. The guards answer by sitting on the ground,
a strike that's paralyzingly effective. I can't differentiate the local
pronunciation of *pastor* from *buster*. Or *bastard*. But it doesn't seem
to matter. Like Washington, DC, Abuja was built in a Federal Capital
Territory, the local tribe herded out to make way. The tree-lined
highway from the airport was renamed Bill Clinton Drive after his
visit. If all he saw were airport, road, and presidential palace, he
must have been impressed. The Nigerian White House is exquisite,
backdropped by an inselberg with silver rivulets streaming down its
face. Neither tragedy nor comedy, where most people live is a
deadpan in-between. The main problem with the urban plan is that
people can drive too fast. I look out the bus window for something
to break the ennui of a left turn against heavy traffic. As our bus
enters the intersection, an oncoming car doesn't notice the
motorcycle tailing us. I can't forget the sickening crack of motorcycle
and skull against asphalt. Traffic stops to gawk. What else can it
do? No doctor, no cop, no space for an ambulance. We drive away
to our meetings and meals. In the hotel restaurant, as soon as we're
seated, a waiter wands the wall-mounted TV on, blaring CNN at us
as if it were life-support. I can't help but wonder what we can
accomplish here. Can't help but think we've already done too little
and, at the same time, too much.

7.

Anyigba

While my colleagues stroll to the bodega for a jerry can of palm
wine, I decide to call it a night. The private bus drives my personal
steward Danladi and me back to my compound, the headlights
interrogating the wan guard, the yard, and the front door of the
house. The entrance teems with insects, every shape and size.
Danladi springs open the padlock, slides the metal bars away from
the door. No petrol for the generator, he hands me matches and a
candle, draws a bucket of water for the bathroom before folding
himself onto the parlor settee, his head propped on its wooden
arm. The night congeals. In the treetops, a bird screeches like a
monkey, or perhaps it's a monkey screeching like a bird. At dawn,
I'm awakened by machetes, a line of sinewed men slashing away
the undergrowth in the yard, calling and responding to keep time.
They're mowing the jungle lawn. Through my window's layers—
bars, screen, glass, lace—I watch them hack and hack.

8.

Lokoja

Yesterday in the rain we said goodbye to Anyigba, goodbye to the rivulets choked with red soil. Goodbye to our darling students grateful for any attention. Goodbye to Darlington, serious Igbo student, dressed in starched shirt and black tie as always, who came to see us off. For him and all the others, I want to return the cheer: *Gbosa! Gbosa! Gbosa!* (When was the last time I was cheered?) For him and all the others—like Yusuf, who shares a dormitory room with four, fills a bucket with the day's worth of water, and studies on the floor—I will cry. I cheer you all with my one word of Igbo, with peanut and kola, with termite saliva, with Maltina, with a bottle of local honey frothing with ground-up bees. Today, we wake in Lokoja, our final stop before descending by bus into the snarled, smoking roads of Lagos. The Governor presents us with souvenirs wrapped in newspaper: ebony masks to hang on our walls. In the gubernatorial hall, our senior colleague crosses the stage to place our official report into the Governor's solemn hands. Polite applause, then *This way*, Pastor whispers, hustling us out of the hall, into the parking lot, and out the back gate, just as a delegation of Bulgarian engineers makes its official entry through the front gate. Clearly, our services to His Excellency the Governor are over. As we wait on sofas in the guesthouse watching CNN without sound, Mr. Innocent Chukwu sits at the table with his ledger, preparing our checks. We hope there will be enough.

ETHIOPIA

LETTER FROM ADDIS ABABA

My friend's brother speeds me through the rows of lavender jacaranda along Bole Road, at each intersection a resistance of beggars. They press against the windows, smack their lips, demonstrating how nothing sounds. They are very young, and at the same time very, very old. My friend's brother stops in front of a shop. *Wait here*, he says. Since then, I spend most of my time in cars. He drops me off inside the Wanza Hotel's walled compound. The guests are an odd lot. For instance, this morning a muscular cow is chained to the gate—today is Coptic Christmas. And there's a Rastafarian from Martinique visiting the land of his resurrected Lord, Haile Selassie, *Ras Teferre*, whose black lions bloat inside concrete and chain-link dens. The music of Bob Marley fits the pace of Addis. At 20, I yearned for that same tropical triumph, to skank in the smell of sweat and honeyed smoke and never ever be spurned. In the cantina, Jean-Michel collapses like a hurt crane when the waiter confiscates his spliff. Two Gulf Arabs stumble out of their room after noon, wearing identical sunglasses, T-shirts and shorts, not quite knowing how to hold the fat cigars they smoke. Tobacco, the denouement after a night of booze and Ethiopian girls, both of which are painfully available. The German aid worker I met on the plane flew into "New Flower" for a similar sniff. The cow is slaughtered in the parking lot. I watch it stagger, fall hard. The bartender spends the day skinning, chunking, grilling. Just before it is done, he douses the sizzling meat with whiskey, inadvertently dissolving his invitation. Instead of eating, I make long-term plans in the shade, watching the guard dog lap up puddles of blood.

ELIAS SNACK

The young waiter in a white lab coat
sidles between tables to ours.

In the din, he whispers the menu—
Engulal. Bunna bi wutat. Dabbo. Mar.

We want to taste them all.
He memorizes our order, flies away,

swoops back. Our breakfast platters
flit from his arm to our table.

When he asks how to reach America,
I wish I were an ambassador

so he could room in our basement,
finish school, marry our daughter,

if she agreed of course.
And why wouldn't she—

such a handsome young man
bearing honey and bread every morning,

who ciphers our bill aloud,
the sum barely audible?

IN EXTREME HOTEL

I already know his name
from his friends caterwauling it
down the corridor while
my wife and children sleep.

I know his home by his tongue,
know this junket he's on
is for gathering human hibiscus,
each night a new bloom.

Through the thin wall,
I know the moment he
plucks her—the rustle,
the mumble, the fall.

He snores. Before dawn,
washing myself for prayer,
I hear her getting dressed.
I hear him remain still.

I know he knows
she's getting ready to leave.
She taps him. They haggle:
More? More? OK? More?

Silence. Click, the door closes.
Her heels pulse down the corridor,
the stairs, past Reception,
through the courtyard

where the old guard
nods on his stool, where
she slips through the creak
in the front gate,

and dissolves into mist.

LETTER FROM DESSIE

The bus spars with us for two days. Punch-drunk, my friend's youngest brother Esihag and I pray Friday Prayer on the mosque courtyard's pointed cobbles. Mornings on his way to primary school, Esihag watched his neighbors wither in the street. The drought lasted two years, orphaned 2,000. Since then, the only English the children learn is *you*, which they shout whenever I'm near. American semis roar through town, a relentless supply of food and clothes. But Muslims must take heed of signs. Perhaps one is the hawk gliding between unclimbable cliffs. Another, that missionaries and aid people rarely get out of their cars. After *fajr* prayer, the imam leads me to the back of the mosque. Kneeling before a screen of yellow sheets, he bids a sound come, and it does: a dozen girls reciting, so soft and steady I want to weep. A beekeeper invites me for breakfast. Entering his simple wooden house, I am met by a thunderous hum: bees attacking the lamp, probing skin, glomming onto the saucer of comb and honey. Imagine sleeping, praying, eating, weeping, all to the drone of Allah's brilliant bees. I no longer believe in beauty unless it thrums in the mouth.

LETTER FROM HAYQ

Muhammad lives in the new blue minaret, the town's highest point overlooking the lake. The mosque soured the man who sells music, so during prayer he blasts Ethiopian pop. *More songs about gonjo*s, his world seems to plead, every tune a beautiful woman on the brink of deciding. If nothing had ever changed, I'd be on a fjord not unlike this narrow lake. Or perhaps I would've already starved. All I mean is I'm not much good at fishing, though I've spent thousands of hours on water. Enjoyed whitecaps too much, and the way weeds slope away under water clearer than morning. Here, the dream fish is trout, stocked by Germans, fried, drizzled with *berbere* and lime. On the way through town, Muhammad pulls up to a small kitchen. A shy girl steps out to the car. Even in Amharic, I know an agreement. She prays privately, Muhammad says, without the knowledge of Copts. If he marries soon, I know the bride. We eat the small, fried trout inside the minaret. Afterwards, the old *muezzin* carves a melon, the slices bright and watery. In my homeland, the fish are longer, fewer, the mosques shorter, fewer still. I spent my childhood near lakes; there were days without speaking. When strange cars came to visit, I hid in the brush. Children here might do the same, provided their bellies are full. When coaxed to say their village's name, they surrender sounds that grace your cheek like a cold wet hand, then crackle like fillets in hot ghee.

LETTER FROM ALEMATA

Abdurehman, my young guide, knows the lingoes: *Tigrinya*, *Amharinya*, *Arabinya* in a pinch. Sitting beside me on the detachable seat over the bus engine, he translates what people are saying as they hand me sticks. It's sugar cane. First, they say, ram your incisors into the end of the stalk. Splinter away the bark. Then crack off pulpy chunks, so full of juice they gush. Maybe it's strange to hear the steps described, but it's the first time my teeth feel like teeth, not the fragile smile crumbling away like pumice in my nightmares. They're delighted I can keep up. We layer the floor with splinters and mark time by counting burned tanks, the mileposts where Tigrayan rebels fought, dug, hunted, all with the same rifle. By the time they reached Addis, their hair had hived, their skin tarred. We reach Alemata at five o'clock, eleven o'clock East African Time. Sometimes I too feel that my life ticks opposite the rest. In this little roadside town, the Phy Ed teacher speaks English, the only resident to have left and returned. At sunset, the three of us walk toward the short minaret, whose little speaker rests inside a crown of sheet metal scraps. To make ablution, dip one plastic cup down into the well, enough water to rub over the limbs like lotion. Inside the green and pink mosque, people congratulate me after deciding I'm not a spy. No spy would travel so far by bus. The more hours I spend riding through the dry landscape, the more I think I'll have their same kind of quiet stories. No jungle colors, but strength in flatness, in dust.

LETTER FROM NEGASH

The asphalt surrenders to gravel, the gravel to fine white dust, and here I am atop a ziggurat hill. The small mosque is locked. From the faucets for ablution come bees. Reading boards etched with short *surah*s in charcoal lean against the wall until children come for their lesson. When I knock on a door, someone hobbles across an inner floor to open it. I've awakened the old *imam* from his nap. His name is Ahmad. He speaks Arabic. Fourteen centuries ago, a small flock of believers brought their hopes here, devout enough to leave their prophet in Mecca. Some died before they could return home. I ask Ahmad to see their graves, but he says no, and won't explain. Then I realize: my camera has made him suspicious. So I offer it to him. He refuses it, but is convinced. He leads me through a graveyard dotted with white pebbles, to a padlocked door, which he unlocks while saying a prayer. He lights sticks of incense, wafts the smoke over a raised portion of floor, under which lie fifteen lives from the time before time started over, along with Negash, King of Aksum, who died on his way to *hajj*. Every life, I suppose, is a *hijrah*. Toward a foreign land. A hopeful hill. A glistening bee.

LETTER FROM HARAR

Here, the powers that be are water and the dead. Even the Ras Hotel boasts only Coke and warm Harar Beer. I am shown around town by Ali. *Half-caste*, he calls himself, Yemen and Ethiopia combined. Ali dredges up a few words of Arabic, not much more than the Old City door, *Bab al-Nasr*. Boogering a smile, he clutches my few *birr* like gold. History makes victims of us all. A snorting, grimy man seizes my arm while a grinning boy plunges his hand into my leg pocket and runs. The man vanishes into the maze of alleys. I chase the boy into the spice market, where Oromo women squat behind sacks of brown powders. But it is like chasing sound. Thankfully, I have nothing to steal. Ali and I enter a few of the 99 mosques, but he never prays. In fact, I haven't seen anyone pray, haven't heard a single *muezzin*. Behind the town, square stones fall into a grid, flee all the way down the valley. More people wait under those unnamed cubes than roofs. Graves aside, there are also children. To them, I'm *Kooba*, *Franjo*, foreign as the Ahmad beneath the black British cross that stands behind the French leper clinic. I'm inconspicuous only at night. Tacked far above towering eucalyptus, the constellations I memorized in middle school pulse. Their names I've neglected to a point their brightness tonight can almost disclose. Each person in the world has a sword. Mine cuts slow, undramatic swaths, the only way I've ever swung at anyone.

FINDING HOME

for Fathia

In Feres Megala, you whirl like a compass,
zero in on the alley between
police station and whorehouse,

count your paces into the mud-brick maze,
down steps stippled with drunkards' piss,
goat and human scat, until you reach

a gate, pound, shout through a crack
till it opens. A boy stands inside, his mother
nodding from the porch behind him to let you in.

You float over the dirt yard to where
you played jacks beneath a tree now
a stump too stubborn to remove,

where you kicked a bundle of leaves
with the side of your foot—how many times
could you send it into the air before you missed?

The ochre house holds not one family
but four, one per room, the walls smudged dark,
decades of children's hands over yours.

BADRIA

sells bread
from a basket
under Shoa Gate

among many
other women, many
other baskets.

I get lost
in the roots
of your family tree

as I'd get lost
in these alleys
of Old Harar

if Badria weren't
leading us from
the gate of bread

to her yard of dirt.
She invites us
inside her small

turquoise room,
rains wrapped toffees
onto our heads.

We stay until we
say we must leave.
Badria sighs,

leads us out to
Feres Megala, the square
where we pry

open the pummeled
door of a taxi,
muscle down a

window and wave
goodbye, Badria,
goodbye.

WHEN FLIES GET STUPID,

Fathia says, *maybe people
will get smart.* But when I
creak open the door

of the neighborhood outhouse,
a cosmos of flies booms
from the black hole.

From first world to third, we lug
heavy hopes for her relatives
though they ask for none.

What miracles bring
dollars, a toolbox, a bale
of used American clothes?

At dusk, the town's most destitute
bed down on cardboard, wrap
themselves in discarded plastic.

When the bathrooms improve,
Fathia says, *now that
will be real progress!*

I place my feet
on the raised bricks
flanking the void, and squat.

YUSEF

At dusk, Yusef sits in his yard
with a bucket of butcher's scraps.

In the headlight of an idling taxi,
he drums the bucket with a eucalyptus twig

until we can see them
leaving the velvet rows of maize,

their eyes smoldering closer
until the alpha female

is standing beside him,
stretching her thick neck toward

his outstretched arm, which
holds the stick, which

dangles a ribbon of flesh.
She peels back her gums,

plucks with careful fangs
the scrap. Scrap after scrap.

But Yusef has a good heart:
as Alpha eats, he flings ribbons

over his shoulder to the others
whining in the periphery.

One of them wanders
into Yusef's open shack,

eyes Yusef's little daughter
playing with a doll on the floor.

But drama is what you fear,
not what is, for Yusef

calls the hyena,
and it comes right out.

BET RIMBO*

Harar

The woman pinning laundry in the yard
points to the stairwell, whose wallpaper

curls with faded bouquets. Upstairs,
in the gutted hall, a matron sits on the floorboards.

Feet bare, legs sprawled in front of her,
she's weaving a small basket in her lap.

She looks up at me, nods permission:
I may step over her legs.

What color did *Ferenji* hear
when hyenas entered the streets after dark

in search of stray dogs? What color
did the day turn when the royal piss

of Menelik II dribbled down
the dome of the Great Mosque?

She doesn't care. But even *Ferenji*
lamented the city was never the same.

Minutes from here, in my hotel,
though the faucets are opened wide,

no water emerges. The floor
of the men's bathroom is splotched

with feces. The ammonia stings my eyes.
In the market I haggle over Adare gold.

I speak Arabic with old men who remember
when words brought prosperity.

I pray in several of the 99 mosques,
one for each of Allah's Beautiful Names.

I drink from the public tin cup.
Drink, *Ferenji*. Tell me what you see.

*Amharic for "Rimbaud's House." Now a museum, *Bet Rimbo* is the house
in which Arthur Rimbaud is purported to have lived during his time in
Harar but most likely did not. See Charles Nicholl's *Somebody Else:
Arthur Rimbaud in Africa, 1880-91*.

LETTER FROM DIRE DAWA

A city is as beautiful as its fruit. Here I've eaten many kinds without knowing their names in any language. The latest one resembled a Granny Smith apple on the outside, but peel it and you get a handful of spun-honey mush around two or three thumbnail-sized seeds. Regarding architecture, imagine Italian colonial storefronts washed in pastel mango, banana, lime, and the ultramarine robes of Michelangelo's Mary. Last night I prayed in a mosque built by Mussolini. Under the blue dome, art-deco arches cascade into pillars. Moorish tiles arabesque the walls. Like the hands that smudge away the walls of other mosques, I wonder if I'll leave anything distinguishable. Sometimes pride whispers from a distance. What achievements will I leave behind? In Taiwan, the local smuggled-goods market, I'm famous. Every Somali and Oromo tailor knows my home state like an inseam. They write down their relatives' phone numbers, and we promise to call them, to let them know that their relative in Dire Dawa is fine. Here, the spaghetti is overcooked, fired with *berbere*, and eaten with fingers from a communal platter. And if someone lifts a robust morsel to your lips, you'd be a fool not to open.

THE BARBER OF TAIWAN

Dire Dawa

My son's hair has begun tickling his ears, so we go for a trim to Taiwan, the market of smuggled everything. Behind the rows of ready-made garments: the row of barbers. The first barber with electric clippers beckons, but my wife isn't taking; she had agreed to the trim on the condition of no electricity, no razor-blade shave around the edges, no nicks. *I didn't return to Ethiopia to give my son HIV*, she says. The electric barber waves his cord toward another lane further in. There, in the lane of scissors, only one barber stall is still open, for lunchtime has begun. My son sits in a folding chair, and the barber turns to us. First, he wipes his scissors with a piece of tissue paper purpled by tincture. Clamping the tissue between the scissor blades, he takes a lighter out of his pocket. I can see the reflection of the flaming scissors in my son's eyes. At my wife's request, I hand the barber my stubby comb compliments of the airline, and he begins clipping and talking. He talks about his hometown to the west, Jimma, as if it were paradise, and maybe it is. Orchards and orchards of tropical fruits. But when the Derg came to round up the young men for conscription, he hid high in a giant tree, swaying with the leaves. The next day, he came here. He works slowly, methodically. We tell him how we want our son's hair to look, but it's no use. The haircut comes out like everybody else's in town.

FROM THE *GARI*

Dire Dawa

The riverbed dividing Kezira
from Megala districts is dry now,
a ribbon of heat, but, the driver says,

faster than you could wake,
rain can fall on distant mountains
and fill it. Imagine the drunk,

the homeless, the itinerant,
the insane, all sleeping
in the softest, most peaceful

bed of their lives suddenly
washed toward the sea.
On a dry shoal, a man bends

over his conundrum. Gaunt,
naked down to a rag, he explains
his logic to a circle of buzzards,

who hang on his every word,
and, when asked, whisper
him the tenderest critique.

AS IF WE SAY MAGIC WORDS

Rift Valley

The Land Rover parts a sea of bony cattle.
Girls with baskets full of unfamiliar fruit press against the windows.

A man drags a giant python by a rope tied behind
the mutilated bulb that was its head.

Through the clouds Lake Abaya peers,
the hem of its skirt stitched by acacia thorns.

On the roadway, we ask the driver to stop
so we can walk down to the edge of the milky water.

Zemzem slips off her flip-flops, rinses her feet.
Our children throw stones so far we can't see them drop.

On the roadway, our driver waves to us with both arms.
We walk back up, where he's standing with two boys,

who say this is the spot where last week
a white couple stopped. All they wanted were photographs.

Focusing her lens on a crocodile, the woman
didn't see the other croc lurking in the periphery.

The husband could do nothing but blink again and again
while his wife disappeared into the milk,

destiny clamped gently to her leg.
In the car, we share prayers for the dead, for the living,

for passing the ridge called the Bridge of God
where lions thunder at dawn,

for reaching the town called Forty Springs
where we fall deeply, deeply asleep.

THE DONKEY

Oromia

As our driver hurtles the Land Rover into the valley,
I see it in a pasture ahead, nipping its friend's bristly mane,
dashing away. How happy their game of tag!
How happy I am! So happy, in fact, that this is where
I want to stop the tale.

But I can't, for never before have I felt such speed
collide with such weight. It soars off the grille guard,
a leather meteorite scudding to a halt on the asphalt,
twitching like a dying insect while its playmate
watches nearby, swishing away flies.

Shepherds appear, balancing staffs across their shoulders.
Small girls walk blankly, arm in arm.
In the lapping stream, mothers lather their babies,
their laundry already slapped against stones
and spread over bushes to dry.

The donkey's owner is in the market, people say,
so our driver rattles down the dirt streets of the nearby village,
asking *Where's the man who owns two donkeys?*
No one knows. What will happen
when he hears the news?

Behind a thicket, the shepherd boy he hired
shrieks without making a sound.
Young men drag the donkey by its stiffened legs
to the edge of the forest, where hyenas
will find it at night. And when the owner

is finally led to the carcass, he wails. How many times
did I tell our driver, *Slow down, for God's sake.*
But all he could think about was racing back to the capital.
In the pasture, elders assemble in a circle under a small tree,
which has become the Tree of Justice.

Our driver presents his case; the donkey's owner, his.
Talk of intention, property, responsibility, compensation
until every point is made. Our driver and the owner
leave. The elders deliberate, and, with a sharpened stick,
scratch the verdict into the dirt.

LETTER FROM ABOARD THE
DJIBOUTI-ADDIS TRAIN

What thoughts we have are avatars. For instance, Adam, the young Somali sitting next to me, chews *chat*, speaks freely in broken English and Arabic until the leaves draw him too deep. Beyond the window stuck open, scrub stunted millennia by cooking fires continues to live, bristling with proud thorns. Long ago, Somalis swam rivers with knives clamped between their teeth, always an eye cocked for crocodile, while their long bodies reached again and again through the water. In those days, even the sorriest excuse of a man wouldn't beat a woman, wouldn't gun down an enemy in prayer until he'd said his last *selam*. After showing me all he had left of his father, the few dog-eared photos, Adam disappeared. But I want him to know that stories live on. They're the red bee-eaters perched on the spines of cattle, and the cumbersome ibises folded onto branches. From them I learn to scan the tops of decapitated trees. The train shifts into another thatch village, halts, surrendering a few minutes for the passengers to buy something for their arrival. Bound live chickens, sugar cane, and sacks of local fruit pass through the windows. Sundown rumbles on blindly toward Nazret, Addis. I can see the silhouettes of people trodding home from work, maybe hours of returning after earning a few *birr*. On the outskirts of the city where I turned around, a man spends his nights dangling meat from his mouth for hyenas. He has become a celebrity, earning a decent wage from tourists. Everywhere, even between two odorous, clamping jaws, lies spectacular destiny.

TUNISIA

STROLLING IN BÉJA, THE EVE OF *AL-MAULID*

for Nabil

People are buying up raisins and salted seeds.
Your father sits at a café table
behind the market, at the end of the alley
with a cigarette, a cup of *crème*,
and a newspaper creased into quarters.

At the government mercantile,
I buy my mother a ceramic hand
decorated with henna flowers.
When I bring it home in a year,
rings that no longer fit her atrophied hand
will slip onto its fingers while unwound watches
will nap across its palm.

We walk on, to the sweet shop
lined with mirrors. On every plate,
a cube of cake soaked with orange-blossom syrup.
Slice it carefully, for if you look
in any direction, you'll find eyes,

everywhere possibility. Our quandary,
mon ami, is that life is a birdcage of glances.
If we escape, we escape on clipped wings
that veer us back to the gate bougainvillea
cascades over, a veranda of cool tile.

Your mother gave you her whiteness.
When I leave the guest room
for the house's more private stations,
I see her sitting at the table with coffee,
her prayer rug facing a bare corner.
Her accent still scurries past me,
but her smile always stops to drink.

Tomorrow, the Prophet Muhammad's birthday.
The daughters of your aunt will visit, wearing pastel dresses.
In the hall, your mother hints you one of them

for marriage. Which one, I can only dream.
A month from now we'll be in a foreign land
where eyes flicker at us from a distance
and this holiday is branded as innovation.

CARTHAGE

At Hannibal Station, I step down
into the stark morning, the train
disappearing toward Tunis. The children

who got off at the same stop
flock to the shop
of the man selling popsicles.

I do not know the way
to the ancient city from which
a battalion marched

until alpine flowers stained
the feet of elephants crimson.
I ask the man, wondering

in which language he will respond.
Up the hill, a colonnade
of stout palms summons no shade.

There, he might point, that way,
down the hill, and I'll find
the stone paths where

Roman children etched games
another day millennia ago,
beyond the flats and railways

of today's children of Carthage,
who flurry past me, laughing
with tongues of orange ice.

CORK

Tunisia

The bus rattles to another halt.

A man boards, swaggers to the back

where other men like him stand.

The bus lurches and lists on,

the men weathering the squalls

like old sailors, not holding on,

not watching the world pass.

Their hawk-nosed knives sway from their belts

until the bus stops and they disappear

into the orchard of stout trunks.

MATMATA

One who views life as a hole digs rooms,
spends years digging. When, over myriad sandstorms,
a purpose other than living still hasn't come,
Allah blows into the pock another pink grain.

Rise meters before most and the morning
will embrace you like a year of arms. The moon:
a cold *qubba* on fading indigo. The sun:
molten bronze pouring in, licking away skin, filling.

Old men climb to the rim, to the small white mosque.
After *fajr*, they praise the Creator of holes.
In the end, no one will be more than salt. Not strange,
not fierce. From Allah comes all that seeps.

Demitasses empty like sentences more lucid in sleep.
News from Gabès crackles from a radio. I have ideas
about what's right: about wool, why clear nights
scour our eyes, what will require more time.

Conquerors can't fill holes, can't do more than billow.
Too often, historians explain us away like hair,
missing how much grit rides wind into teeth,
how few curses hide inside stone tongues. One.

The sun once again renders holes dismal. A homely girl
beats sand across a *howsh*. A tethered camel bawls
at her brother climbing out for water. Their father dreams
of whitening hands, while their mother, in an inner hole, digs.

CHOTT EL-DJERID

for Nabil

Beyond our bus window, a man sinks
a crowbar into the salt crust.
The arm of brown crystals he dislodges
he'll hawk along the roadside
beneath a big hand-painted sign.

The bus stops. Its door accordions open
for several old women who clink and jangle
into the stairwell and the seats behind the driver.
The lines tattooed between their chins and lower lips
speak a language of branches teeming with green finches.

You and I talk.
We go silent.
The bus stops again. The women
step down, crunch toward the mountains
drifting back and forth like curtains.

The bus continues on
toward the oasis where date palms
clatter their orange nodes, where
a pair of earrings once jangled,
and you were born.

SAUDI ARABIA

THE ARABIAN ORYX

In his Suspended Ode, a 6th-century poet says, *A young oryx, / circlet of silver and black onyx jangling on her forehead, / hastens to the safety of her mother / to nibble sprigs of sage.*

The Kingdom of Saudi Arabia is four times the size of France.

In the Kingdom, traffic accidents are the largest cause of death among foreigners.

I want to drive from Jeddah to Taif to see the Arabian oryx captive breeding program, but I am afraid of dying.

I choose not to drive in the Kingdom, so each morning my university-appointed chauffeur phones me when he's in the street in front of my apartment building. He speeds me to the Faculty of Arts and Humanities at King Abdulaziz University as if someone's life depended on it.

The arrows of destiny don't miss their target.

At King Abdulaziz University, there are parallel campuses, segregated by sex.

In 1990, my classes at Sana'a University in Yemen are coed. In my Beginning English class of 88 students, 63 are female.

Of those 63 female students, 45 wear full veils. Two of them are named *Maha*, which is Arabic for "oryx." Pronouncing their names, I see their eyes meet mine for a split-second before darting away.

In Oman in 1972, hunters in a four-wheel-drive Toyota run down and shoot the last wild Arabian oryx.

She turns upon them with her horns, like the sharp, strong spears of Semhar.

For the next decade, Arabian oryx exist only in captivity.

Her eyes are two sparrows / chirping outside a window of alabaster.

In 1982, Arabian oryx specimens from zoos and royal menageries are joined to create a "world herd," which is reintroduced into the wilds of Oman.

The Sultanate of Oman trains and employs local Harasis tribesmen as rangers to protect the Arabian oryx, which roam inside the Arabian Oryx Sanctuary, an unfenced area the size of Belgium.

The number of Arabian oryx in Oman grows to 450. The story of their success inspires conservationists worldwide.

The Sultanate of Oman does not include the Janaba, a neighboring tribe that outnumbers the Harasis three to one, in Arabian oryx conservation.

In 1996, animal collectors from the Gulf begin offering cash to the Janaba to poach Arabian oryx from the Harasis' sanctuary. A live female Arabian oryx fetches up to $20,000.

Her legs / the smooth pillars of a lofty castle.

Many Arabian oryx are captured and sold alive to millionaires with private menageries. Some die from injuries sustained during abduction. Others are found dead in the desert, their legs bound.

Is my camel like an Arabian oryx / sheltering her calf from hunters?

By 2007, the number of Arabian oryx in Oman dwindles to 65, only four of which are female.

The Sultan decrees that the Arabian Oryx Sanctuary will be reduced from the size of Belgium to a fenced area of 1.5 square miles, which will be guarded by police patrols armed with automatic weapons.

When the glittering sands dance at noon, / and the hills don the gowns of mirage, / I will accomplish my desire.

In villages near Marib, Yemen, houses are built with stone blocks pilfered from ancient Sheban ruins, some of which display bas-reliefs of Arabian oryx.

I walk through dusty alleys looking for oryx on the walls of homes until children pelt me with stones.

I am not one to sulk behind a hilltop, / but I am haunted by dark eyes ringed with kohl.

DREAMS BEACH

Jeddah, Saudi Arabia

My teenage daughter and I surrender our passports at the compound's door, lug our rented diving gear past the Indian servants hosing down the tropical flowers, past the Lebanese apollos playing beach volleyball, past the hookah bar wafting strawberry smoke over the pool, past the bikini-clad Moroccan girl shimmying to her Saudi boyfriend's boom box, to the end of the pier pounded by waves. She hesitates—no other females are snorkeling, just rotund young men wearing wetsuits and air tanks, gawking at her pink bodysuit, their gaze heavy and silent as a full moon. I cling to the cement landing while securing my fins, mask, and snorkel between each crash of wave. And then I bend forward, stick my face into the warm salt froth, and, believe it or not, fish are darting around my knees—blue, yellow, and orange, like a saltwater aquarium, and beyond them lie corals, some dead and gray, others glowing green, pink. I call to my daughter; she descends the ladder and takes my hand. I hold her elbow so she isn't washed away, her first time in the sea's give and take. I ask her if she's ready to push away, and she is. Arm in arm, we kick and float through the coral corridors while the Saudi boys with weighted belts bubble on the bottom. See that school of fish that look like rainbows, she points. See that neon-blue fish with a yellow tail, curled inside that grotto, I point. Butterfly, parrot, clown, trigger, pipe, lion—back and forth we point and point at each moment of real beauty before it flashes away.

LETTER TO THE SAUDI TEEN WHO THREW
HIS PHONE NUMBER TO MY DAUGHTER

Jeddah, Saudi Arabia

My Dear Boy,

As you can see, I'm not escorting my wife and daughter on their walk along the sea today. I have some work to complete, and I know they can manage themselves. They hail a taxi, ride it to the start of Palestine Street, and walk north along the Corniche, the warm breeze blowing off the Red Sea, the giant offshore fountain spewing mist over the bay. They snap photos of each other beside the giant abstract sculptures punctuating the sidewalk. They pass Egyptian laborers, who, during off-time, cast hooks baited with smashed crabs into the greasy waves. And when they tire of walking, they rest on benches, watching through their sunglasses people stroll. A Sudanese woman offers to flourish my daughter's feet with henna.

By sunset, they pass the luxury hotels, the manmade lagoon, the pricey Lebanese restaurant, all the way to the Floating Mosque, where they pray on the pillared veranda, the surf crashing beneath. After *maghrib* prayer, vendors sell toys that flash and whirl in the twilight. My wife and daughter begin their return, passing boys who sell rides on tasseled ponies, and kids who zoom kick-scooters around their Filipina nannies.

And when they rest again on a bench, a group of teenage boys begins singing, their skinniness accentuated by tailored white gowns. You are one of them, the rake cocking his scarf high on the back of his head, its tail flowing in the breeze like a stallion's. You've got a good voice, the Arabic love song you sing mellifluous yet brassy enough to cut through the white noise and reach the ears of my daughter. You walk past her bench serenading the night, and, with pinpoint accuracy, flick a tiny paper wad against her slipper.

I applaud your aim, your taste. But my daughter ignores your love pellet. She's new to the kind of clandestine rendezvous you throb for, the soap-opera whisper from a receiver, the promises no one expects you to keep. She doesn't respond.

You give up, move on, for there are many other girls under the invisible stars. Then, pretending to scratch her foot, my daughter picks up your note, drops it into her '*abaya*'s deep pocket. Home, she tells me the whole story, dropping your paper pill into my palm. I unroll it: a thin strip ripped from a school notebook, a mobile number scrawled in faint pencil. I almost want to call, to say I'm sorry for the lengths you must go to, sorry that after such a splendid scene my daughter won't be starring in your romantic comedy. Perhaps if I'd escorted her, you wouldn't have wasted your time. I know how it is: a night ticks away like a lifetime of second hands. And really, I'm glad you sing on the sidewalk instead of trolling the boulevard in a Maserati. I know how dangerous the roads are, especially if you're distracted by the moonlight dancing on the waves, eluding touch, never returning the call.

AMERICA

CURING

for my mother

I return from the Orient with medicines:
poultices, unguents, pungent seeds, honey
robust and raw, specked with the limbs of bees.

I return to visit you in the hilltop cabin,
where your hand tingles away like the fingers
of steam reaching out of the lake on a cool morning.

The folk healer held little hope: too many years,
too much radiation, too many pills strong enough
to be poison. The best medicine is prayer, he said,

handing me vials of black cumin seeds and sesame oil
to warm and massage over your arm.
The combination might stimulate the nerves, he said,

if they aren't already damaged beyond repair.
So that is what I am doing. When I was two, maybe three,
I stood in this same kitchen, watching Dad scorch bacon

each morning until you returned, your elbow tucked
into the new hollow of your chest. So I rub the warm grit
over your arm, milking the flesh from the elbow downward.

It's tingling, you say, as I cap the vials.
We'll repeat the treatment twice a day until the contents are gone,
until there is nothing, absolutely nothing left inside.

STILL

for Soheil Najm in Baghdad

Americans still sigh in sorrow.

Americans seem sorry in their sorrow.

*Sorry. . .sorrow. . .*syllables stamped flat

like sides of a coin, one holding

a president's head, the other a ruin

or flattened eagle. Sorry for thinking

about coins. Sorry for the sorrow

brimming its banks like the Tigris,

for shrapnel ribboning blood vessels,

for a door splintering through

a nephew's heart. Thinking of you,

I picture a tumbler of chilled

karkadeh, the crimson infusion

of hibiscus flowers picked during

their one and only day of bloom.

Sometimes, all one has

is a day, a sorry little word.

WILD ROSES

with versions of Eastwick's translation of Sa'di's *Gulistan*

A century ago, this narrow shelf on the hill
halfway between cabin and lake
was a logging road. Now, it bristles with wild roses.

I visited a hermit in Bilqan

I'm digging them up because I love them,
their vigor, their marriage of passion and pain.
I want them with me, in the city.

to ask him for enlightenment.

Severing their underground cords, I plunge the mother-plants
into buckets of water so they won't wilt. Why do I pamper
brambles nearly impossible to kill?

"Professor, be patient like dirt," he advised,

For three hours, they ride in the back seat while forests,
lakes, and farms blur past. In the front yard, I stuff them into holes
under the big blue spruce, where nothing else grows.

"or else you might as well bury your texts."

They wilt. But wilting does not necessarily end a story.
After several days, the bare canes slowly unfurl
makeshift green flags. The revolution has begun.

For how many years, for how many long lives

If every living thing is a clock, don't wear a watch.
In spring they wave their gloved hands
like girls in a small-town parade a century ago.

will people walk on the ground above my head?

A young farmer waits outside the one-room school
until he can hand the new schoolteacher a wild rose.
She presses it inside the leather cover of *Victorian Verse*.

From hand to hand the land was passed to us,

A century later, I find my grandmother's book,
the brown floral splay staining the pages,
in a musty box in the basement.

and on it will go to other hands.

By autumn, the honeymoon has passed.
Their hips swell red, life bearing life.
The smell of dried sweat.

It's not right that people, created from earth,

In the bitterest cold week of January,
cottontails clip off a few
of their thorny red stalks.

puff up with pride, violence, and gas.

Each year, they calculate their advance
across the lawn, following subterranean
communiqués, shooting up pink flares.

You display so much heat and stubbornness,

Too many root-ropes underground,
too many spiny shoots.
They've got to go. I'm overrun.

you must be made of fire instead.

HOLIDAY LIGHTS

Fargo

The neighbor's house down the street throbs like a jackpot:
blue lights pacing along gutters, candy canes and stockings
high-kicking from the windows, Santa and reindeer
flashing red on the peak. In the yard, the snow so fluffy and clean

it challenges belief, a life-size crèche glows like a display
of giant lava lamps. My seven-year-old son Abdu,
born in Arabia, asks, "Daddy, why do they have Muslims
in their yard?" And sure enough, there is the Virgin

Maryam, her whole body, even her hair, draped in blue *chador*,
while bearded men in turbans and long gowns gaze with her
at the baby 'Eisa wrapped in an immaculate rag,
everyone so aglow with bulbs inside that I have to wonder

what is being proclaimed: the more lit, the more free?
In Afghanistan, bombs the size of Volkswagens
cut into mountains. How lovely a million lights
must look from above. In a Quranic parable, olive oil

glows amber within a lamp whose flame glows within a glass flue,
the flue glowing within a niche, the niche lighting a dark corner.
This exponential glow is what Allah is. O bungalow in snow,
your lights are gaudy and cold, your television bodes death

for seven million foreigners this winter. So I send a check.
My son sacrifices two dollars from his commemorative quarter collection.
This year, he has learned to pledge his allegiance and sing "Jingle Bells."
With his American grandparents he eats turkey at Thanksgiving.

He is thankful for candy. Swimming pools. Batteries. Forgive me,
Allah, if I sound cynical. I must remember that it is Ramadan and I am fasting,
that this month words should be kind and tempered, words should be
peaceful unless, of course, they are necessary for one's defense.

Glossary

'abaya: a loose-fitting overgarment worn by women.

Adare: the tribe originally from Harar.

Amharinya: the Amharic language.

ameen: the Arabic-Islamic equivalent of "amen."

Arabinya: the Arabic language.

berbere: traditional Ethiopian chili powder.

bet: house.

birr: Ethiopian currency.

bunna bi wutat: coffee with milk; latté.

chat: the Ethiopian name for a mildly narcotic plant cultivated in the Red Sea region and chewed socially. (see also *qat*).

dabbo: bread.

Derg: the Communist politburo that ruled Ethiopia from 1975 to 1987.

diwan: a sitting room, often with cushions lining the walls.

duqq: a variety of spiced Yemeni coffee.

engulal: eggs.

fajr: pre-dawn; one of the five daily Islamic prayer times.

ferenji/Franjo: literally "Frankish"; a term for a foreigner.

gari: a horse-drawn carriage used as local transportation in Dire Dawa and some rural areas of Ethiopia.

gonjo: beautiful girl.

hajj: the pilgrimage to Mecca.

howsh: small courtyard.

imam: the prayer leader.

kohl: black powder used as mascara.

Kooba: literally "Cuba"; a term for a foreigner, originating from the 1970s and 1980s when Cuba dispatched soldiers to Ethiopia to support its Communist ambitions.

maghrib: sunset; one of the five daily Islamic prayer times.

mar: honey.

Merkato: vast open-air market in Addis Ababa.

muezzin: the person who calls Muslims to their five daily prayers.

mujahed: literally, "one who struggles or strives." Specifically, those Muslims who fought the Soviet forces in Afghanistan in the 1980s.

qat: the Arabic name for the mildly narcotic plant cultivated in the Red Sea region and chewed socially. (see also *chat*).

qubba: dome.

Ras Teferre: literally "the Awe-Inspiring Head"; an epithet of King Haile Selassie I.

rial: Yemeni currency.

selam: literally "peace"; a greeting in both Amharic and Arabic; what is said at the close of a Muslim's prayer.

souq: market.

Souq al-Nisa': "the Women's Market"; the region of the market where women's clothing and accessories are sold.

surah: a chapter of the *Qur'an*, Islam's holy book.

Tigrinya: the Tigrayan language.

Yahya Frederickson teaches writing and literature at Minnesota State University Moorhead. He holds an MFA in Creative Writing from the University of Montana and a PhD in English from the University of North Dakota. Between graduate degrees he taught for six years in Yemen, initially as a Peace Corps Volunteer. He has served as a Fulbright Scholar in Syria, Saudi Arabia, and Kyrgyzstan.

He is the author of *The Gold Shop of Ba-'Ali*, which won Lost Horse Press's 2013 Idaho Prize. He's also the author of four chapbooks. The latest chapbook, *The Birds of Al-Merjeh Square: Poems from Syria*, won the 2013 Open Chapbook Competition at Finishing Line Press. His other chapbooks are *Month of Honey, Month of Missiles* (Tigertail, 2009), *Returning to Water* (Dacotah Territory, 2006) and *Trilogy* (Dacotah Territory, 1985, with Julie Taylor and Richard Schetnan).

His poems have appeared in *Arts & Letters, Black Warrior Review, Clackamas Literary Review, Crab Orchard Review, Cream City Review, CutBank, Cutthroat: A Journal of the Arts, Flyway, Great River Review, Green Mountains Review, Hanging Loose, The Laurel Review, Midwestern Gothic, Mizna, Ninth Letter, Prairie Schooner, River Styx, Quarter After Eight, Quarterly West, The Southern Review, WLA, Water~Stone Review, Witness*, and other journals.

His translations (with Muhammed Shoukany) of contemporary Saudi Arabian poets appear in *New Voices of Arabia: The Poetry: An Anthology from Saudi Arabia* (I.B. Tauris, 2012).

CPSIA information can be obtained
at www.ICGtesting.com
Printed in the USA
BVOW08s1942200117
474077BV00001B/9/P